How To Hop-Up and Customize Your Harley-Davidson Softail

Timothy S. Remus

Published by:
Wolfgang Publications, Inc.
217 Second Street North
Stillwater, MN 55082
www.wolfpub.com

Legals

First published in 2005 by Wolfgang Publications, Inc.
217 Second Street North, Stillwater MN 55082

© Timothy Remus, 2005

ISBN number: 1-929133-22-7

Printed and bound in the USA

Advanced Custom Painting Techniques

Acknowledgements

This is getting to be a bad habit. Work Saturday, work Sunday, all in an effort to get the book to the distributor when it's only three or four weeks late. Near the very end there's always the "oh shit," moment, "I forgot to write the Intro and the Acknowledgements."

Let me start by thanking the four resident experts (see Chapter Two) Arlen Ness, Dave Perewitz, Donnie Smith, and Paul Yaffe, all of whom sat still long enough that I could do a short interview, and then sent photos of bikes and products. For explaining the finer points of billet wheel manufacture I thank John Trutnau at PMFR.

Various members of V-twin aftermarket helped with images and advice. A partial list would include Cycle-Visions, Drag Specialties, Klock Werks, Arlen Ness Inc, Kuryakyn, Dakota Digital, PM, Progressive, Russ Wernimont, and Lee Wimmer (Wimmer Custom Cycle).

Photo sequences of real people performing real service on real motorcycles is the best way to explain a particular operation, but shooting such a sequence involves the cooperation of the shop and mechanic. For inviting me and my always intrusive camera into their shops I thank the following shops: Dougz, PMFR, Shadley Brothers, World Class Tuning (Doug Lofgren), Lee's Speed Shop, Kangas Enameling, Kokesh MC and American Thunder. Neil at American Thunder, Doug at Dougz and Kevin at Lemans come in for special mention as they really went the extra mile to get the Project Softail bike finished in time to meet the book deadline. To round out the list I need to thank Gene Slater for last-minute bike photos and Doug Mitchel and Greg Field for additional historical photos.

Our resident design expert Jacki Mitchell gets a tip of the hat for the nice photos and clean layout of this fine book. For paying the bills (and Jacki) and acting as my favorite "filter" I thank Krista Leary. And last but not least, thanks to my lovely and talented wife Mary Lanz – for over twenty years of patience and proof reading.

Introduction

If ever an American company designed and brought to market a killer product, it was and is the Softail from Harley-Davidson. Introducing a good product is as much about timing as the product itself. In the case of the Softail, the new model came at a time when it was once again very cool to drive and use American products. By styling it to look like an old Hardtail, The Company tapped into a bottomless pit of yearning for American Nostalgia. The fact that the new bike came with a new engine, one that didn't leak oil or require mechanical skills for ownership, didn't hurt.

Most new bike owners, Softail owners in particular, can't wait to personalize their bike. We all want them faster, sexier and lower. With those goals in mind we've put together this Hop Up & Customizing guide. There are no hard and fast rules here, but there are guidelines and suggestions from our team of experts like Donnie Smith, Dave Perewitz, Paul Yaffe and Arlen Ness. Follow their advice on the things you should and should NOT do – and save some money at the same time.

It's all about value. Anyone can have a really cool bike by dropping off the bike and a bag full of cash at one of the customizers just mentioned. More difficult is the goal of designing and building a cool bike on limited funds and no professional help.

Like all big jobs, the idea of building a cool bike is less intimidating if you break it down into smaller segments. Thus we provide information on Design, the Chassis, Wheels & Brakes, Sheet Metal & Paint, Accessories, Engine work and a full Bike Assembly.

Too many of us run right out and buy a garage full of accessories the same day we buy the bike. Six months later we begin to realize that given the second chance to spend that Accessory budget, we would do it much differently. The goal then is to wait, to think, before spending more on chrome stuff than you did on the bike.

In addition to time, money and a brain, there's at least one more thing you need to customize that Softail – a good service manual. We've tried to include things like torque specs and step-by-step procedures in this book, but we simply haven't, and couldn't, include them all. A service manual holds a wealth of information for anyone really interested in their motorcycle. From the amount and type of oil to use in the transmission, to the proper sequence for head-bolt removal.

Now you know what you need, the rest as they say, is up to you.

Chapter One

Softail History

The Bike That Saved Milwaukee

What we think of as a Harley-Davidson Softail might also be called one of the better industrial designs of all time. Consider how many objects stay in production for over twenty years, how many cars last more than two or three model years. And how many of those get credit for saving the company from the jaws of waiting creditors.

HISTORY

For anyone who's forgotten their history, Harley-Davidson bought themselves back from

When it comes to capturing the magic and allure of a bygone era, no one does it better than Harley-Davidson. Doug Mitchel

AMF in June of 1981, just in time to enjoy the deep slide in motorcycle sales as an independent company without access to AMF's deep pockets. Just because money was tight doesn't mean the crew in Milwaukee wasn't working on new ideas. Design of an up-dated engine started while AMF was still writing the checks. Though the prototypes were finished by the time of the buy out, finishing up all the details and getting the new engine ready for production became the responsibility of the new Harley-Davidson company.

Harley-Davidson created the first Softail by mating the then-current Wide Glide chassis with the new pseudo Hardtail rear frame section. Greg Field Collection

Intended as an evolutionary upgrade on the Shovelhead, the new engine we now know as the Evo used aluminum cylinders instead of cast iron, eliminating problems with the different expansion rates that occur between the Shovel's aluminum cases and cast iron cylinders. By using long through studs anchored in the cases the structural load was taken off the cylinders, which makes for a stronger engine, and less cylinder distortion during operation. As a cylinder material aluminum has the added benefit of shedding heat much more readily than cast iron. What really separates the Evo from the Shovel, however, is head design. Where the Shovel uses a big combustion chamber shaped like the legendary hemi, the Evo uses a more compact D-shaped chamber. Additional differences in the two heads include narrower

The first Softails, introduced in 1984, came to the party with the then-current four-speed transmissions. That funny appendage seen hanging on the right side of the transmission in the upper photo is a kick starter. Greg Field Collection

Detail shot shows the design of the early swingarm and the chain drive. Greg Field Collection

By 1986, the Softail line included a new model, the Softail Custom with the frame painted to match the sheet metal. The belt drive and five-speed tranny came in 1985. Greg Field Collection

valve angles and redesigned ports.

Not only do the new heads breathe better than the old, they're much more efficient and less prone to detonation. The smaller chamber gives up less heat (and power) to the aluminum that shapes the combustion chamber. The D-shape also means the piston comes up and almost touches a shelf on the flat side of the D. The mixture that's forced out from under the shelf creates the swirl needed to help mix the fuel and air and distribute the mixture through the combustion chamber.

Though it's called an Evo and shares the basic architecture with the old Shovelhead, the newer V-twin engine is revolutionary in many ways. The Shovelhead came with issues, all of which were addressed by the Evo. When the Evo came on line the old problems with oil consumption, detonation and oil leakage went away.

In addition to making the new Evo engine ready for production, Harley-Davidson spent the early 1980s developing two new chassis. One, the FXR, was really a smaller version of the rubber-mount FLTC chassis, first introduced in 1980. The other new frame was a little different, both in its style and in the source of the original design.

THE FIRST SOFTAIL

We've all heard the stories about the first Softail, how some non-Harley-Davidson guy designed a frame with the shocks and springs under the transmission which created the bike what everybody wanted – the looks of a hardtail without the harsh ride. Most of the story is true, depending of course on which version you've heard. The guy's name is Bill Davis, an engineer, mechanic and bike nut from St. Louis. Bill started with a triangular swingarm, supported by springs under the seat and a pivot about halfway down the forward leg of the triangle. In 1976 he offered the design to Harley-Davidson. When they came back with an offer he considered too low, Bill formed a company to manufacture the frames. To make a long story short, Bill eventually moved the shock/spring units under the transmission, which made for a more pleasing package in a visual sense but did nothing to ensure his financial success. Like nine out of ten start-up companies, the new manufacturer of the "Sub Shock" frame eventually went bust. In despair Bill called Willie G. Davidson one more time.

This is a story with a happy ending. As you know, Willie said yes, and Bill began receiving royalties. In fact Bill ended up working as a consultant to Milwaukee.

First Factory Softail

Once they purchased the rights from Bill, along with six completed frames, the engineering department at Harley-Davidson put the pedal to the metal to get the frame ready in record time. It took them eighteen months to go from prototypes to finished frames ready for production. Timing of the new frame couldn't have been better, at least in the sense that the new frame was ready for prime time at the same time as the new engine.

For the 1984 model year Harley spread the risk of introducing a new engine by equipping some bikes with the Evo and others with the

The first prototype frames built by Bill Davis put the springs under the seat with a small shock absorber mounted between them. Greg Field Collection

Bill Davis poses with some early Sub Shock frames. Greg Field Collection

9

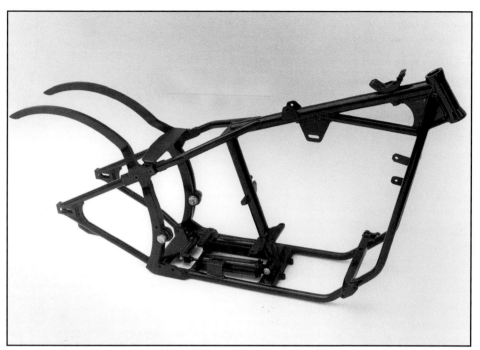

One of Bill's early Sub Shock frames with the urethane shock absorbers - looks amazingly close to early factory frames. Greg Field Collection

This rare bird, a Shovelheaded Softail, is one of Bill's early prototypes. Greg Field Collection

Shovelhead. As a new model, it made sense to equip the Softail with the new engine. The first Softails came to market looking like a Wide Glide (FXWG), twenty-one inch front wheel and all, except of course for the new "hard-tail" section grafted on at the back. We all know what happened. Equipped with the new Evo engine, a four-speed transmission, and chain drive to the rear wheel, the Softail became the bike to own.

Not only did the Softail sell and sell well, the Softail also became a bike the factory could morph into an entire family of bikes all based on the same chassis. By 1985 the chain final drive made way for a belt, and one year later Harley-Davidson introduced the first two spin-offs from the original Softail, the Softail Custom and the Heritage Softail. The Custom was in fact the Softail that might have emerged from the local custom shop of the day. The spoked rear wheel made way for a disc wheel, lots of chrome was added, and the frame was painted with the same Candy Burgundy paint used for the sheet metal.

There are certain good things about growing old. In the case of Harley-Davidson it meant being able to mine your own history for styling cues to use again on new motorcycles. The Heritage moved the whole model line and the company forward by looking back, back to the 1949 Hydra-Glide. Though the bike looked old, it shared the new-to-the-Softail-line five-speed transmission. Which meant a slight redesign of the frame, including a new forged frame member under the seat, the part of the frame that contains the swingarm pivot, often called the boomerang.

More mining unearthed an old fork design known as the Springer. Modern materials meant the pivot points on the fork would last more than one riding season. A freshening of the original design meant four inches of travel from a very compliant fork assembly. The first-year Springer came complete with a front fender setup high enough off the tire to make the bike qualify as a motocross bike. As always the situation improved two years later when the moto-fender was moved closer to the tire by means of a clever linkage connecting the fork to the fender.

The next birth to the Softail family arrived looking rather rotund and pretty much unlike any of the other siblings. Instead of bold striking colors, the bike came in monochromatic silver. Rather than use spoked wheels the new kid came with solid wheels on both ends. Fat Boy seemed the only logical name for what would be one of the most successful members of the Softail family.

It seems Willie and crew could do no wrong with variations on the Softail theme. One success begat another and another. In addition to Fat Boys, Willie and crew gave us Bad Boys, Night Trains and another Springer called the Springer Heritage.

A SMALL WRINKLE IN A PERFECT PIECE OF SHEET METAL

If a design can be judged purely by its success in the marketplace the Softail, as introduced in 1984 and manufactured through the 1990s, was as perfect as they come. Hell, people waited in line for two and three years just to own a new one.

If the Softail had a flaw, that flaw was vibra-

Like the Softail Custom, the first Heritage was another stroke of genius introduced in 1986. Greg Field Collection

The Heritage borrowed heavily from Harley's past, specifically the 1949 Hydra-Glide complete with passing lamps and the fork tin. Greg Field Collection

In the Good Old Days, Indians came with a Girder front end and Harleys came with a Springer. It was only natural then to re-create and update the Springer and hang it on the front of the Softail Chassis. Doug Mitchel

Though it looks to some like a motorcycle in need of paint and billet wheels, the Fat Boy became another run-away best seller for Harley-Davidson. Doug Mitchel

tion. Unlike the Dresser or rubber-mount FXR and Dyna bikes, the engine in a Softail bolts directly to the frame, transmitting vibrations directly to the rider. Despite what the old-timers say, vibration is at best a pain in the ass, and at worst a prime cause of rider fatigue. Some riders predicted a rubber-mounted Softail frame, but Harley-Davidson, being Harley-Davidson, took another route entirely. A Counter-Balanced Twin Cam.

In 1998 Harley-Davidson introduced the new Twin Cam engine. But the really big news in the Twin Cam department came one year later when Milwaukee introduced a second model of the Twin Cam – one with counter balancers designed to eliminate vibration instead of simply isolating it with rubber engine mounts.

The new Twin Cam, designated B, was designed for one reason, to eliminate the vibrations in a Softail without resorting to a rubber engine mounting system. In the case of the new-for-2000 Softails, people have said that, "Harley changed everything and they changed nothing. They gave us a motorcycle with both a new frame and engine, one that looked pretty much just like the old motorcycle. Only in America!"

If you look closely at the B-model Twin Cam found in late model Softails, the cases are a little different than they are on a Dyna or Dresser. The new softail still bolts the engine directly to the frame, but in reality the engine hangs on "axles" that go from one side of the frame, through the case and out the other side. Instead of using an engine and separate transmission like Softails did for fifteen years, the new Softail bolts the transmission up directly to the rear of the engine. The two mate so closely they are in effect one assembly. This means there's no room for the standard under-seat vertical frame tube.

The biggest single change in the new and old Softail frames is the missing under-seat tube. Yes, there is a tube, but it's a bolt -in member not an integral part of the frame.

In terms of installing a Twin Cam in an Evo powered frame, it can be done, but only if you use the A version of the Twin Cam mated up to the standard early-style five-speed transmission. The rear motor mounts, missing on a Twin Cam, can be "installed" through use of an adapter available from the aftermarket. Because the engine mounts are so different, there is no easy way to install a B version of the new engine in an early-style frame.

If the new Softail frame and Evo engine teamed up to save Milwaukee's best, the counter-balanced Twin Cam and new Softail frame have likewise teamed up to ensure that success well into the new millennium.

With the new Twin Cam engine came a completely new frame, which at first glance looks a lot like the old frame. Shown is another Softail spin off, the Night Train.

The revolution never stops. It was only a matter of time before Harley-Davidson would stuff a 200 tire under a Softail fender and gave it a 103 inch engine for power .

Chapter Two

Planning & Design

Good News/Bad News

First, the good news: The Softail model comes in a wide variety of models, From the stripped Standard and Night Train models, to fully fendered Fat Boys and Heritage bikes. Add a set of bags and windshield to a Heritage or Fat Boy and you've created a light touring bike. Which brings us to the bad news: Because the Softail comes in so many different models and styles, there are literally hundreds of ways to customize a Softail.

So let's start by generalizing on the topic of

Aaron Mentele's Fat Boy takes on a muscular stance with 18 inch PM wheels and brakes. The simple black and chrome treatments never go out of style. A 180 rear tire is stuffed up into the stock swingarm, with fender and struts from the Klock Werks shop. Front fender is from Jesse James, flush-mount axle from Dakota Billet. Power comes from a 95 inch engine with HQ heads and ignition. Gene Slater

customizing, or making the bike your very own. The catalogs, from Drag Specialties or Harley-Davidson, are filled to the brim with accessories designed for Softails. And of course, the Factory offers more of the same, everything from flamed grips to new bars, seats, windshields and luggage. Though the offerings from Harley-Davidson might be more conservative than what's found in the aftermarket catalogs, the parts are generally of very high quality, available at your local dealer, and in many cases (like the Deuce saddlebags and many of the sheet metal items) can be ordered with color-matched paint.

Another Fat Boy from Klock Werks, Jennifer's bike retains the stock colors and stock tank. And again, no frame changes. Brian and crew added the nacelle, flush-mount axle and K-W front fender. Dan Cheeseman extended the stock rear fender, added smooth struts and fabbed a nifty taillight. G. Slater

Before ordering the flamed grips from the local dealer and a new set of deeply chromed forward controls from Custom Chrome, however, ya gotta think about what it is you're trying to create here.

The goal (at least for most of us) is a bike with a certain visual impact. One that's different from all the others out there. A bike with pleasing lines, one that sits "just right." All the chrome stuff from the catalogs will not, by themselves, make such a bike.

Which means ya gotta think. Think about your goals for the bike. Think about the paint. Think about your budget. In fact, the budget should probably be the first item on the read-this-first list. If the budget is tight, there's no sense designing a killer bike with a five-thousand dollar paint job

Jennifer Mentele's ride rolls on 18 inch wheels from Xtreme Machine, wrapped in Metzeler tires. Chrome additions include the swingarm, license plate bracket from Heartland and a variety of smaller items. To quote Mr. Klock, "Stock can rock." Gene Slater

Mike Crawley's Softail might be called a work-in-progress. What started as a Softail Standard is now a sharp looking hot rod, thanks mostly to a wide tire kit from American Thunder. Sheet metal changes include the extended gas tank, the rear fender (part of the kit) and aftermarket front fender.

After modifying the stock seat pan, Mike built and upholstered his own seat. Future plans include more engine work and a billet front wheel to match the rear - both the rear wheel and drive side brake are from PMFR.

and six thousand dollar engine upgrade. Either devise a plan that gets the job done for an amount you can spend, or one that progresses in steps so you can upgrade as you go.

Figure out how much of the work you can do yourself, and budget for the things that can't be done in the home garage. Riders who live in cold country might want to have big items like engine work or a paint job done in the winter when the bike is laid up anyway. Some shops even offer lower labor rates (or free storage) for work done during the winter.

The important thing is to decide what it is you want, both in terms of visual items like paint and sheet metal, and more mechanical items like engine hop ups and suspension work. Put a price on each item (including labor), add a fudge factor, and then modify the overall plan so it fits the family budget. Before disregarding the planning phase of the project, consider that it's too easy to just throw money at a bike. To buy some little trinket every week without considering how all the trinkets work together. It's a better use of limited funds to figure out ahead of time the best way to create the desired effect.

The three biggest single items for most builders are: paint, engine work and trick wheels. A custom paint job can easily cost three, four or five thousand dollars. Bumping the displacement to 95 cubic inches, with new cams and all the rest will set you back a similar amount. Item three in the "expensive items" list might be wheels, tires and brakes. As you can see by looking over the Gallery bikes, a set of wheels with matching brakes really helps to set a custom Softail apart from all the rest, yet the cost is substantial.

Project Softail, seen in this book, is our own attempt to build a Bobber from a late model Softail. The idea is to provide an idea bike for Softail owners looking for a project that doesn't require gobs of money and/or fabrication. Note first that the bike is a Standard, the least expensive Softail. Note too, that the concept would work equally well on a Springer or Night Train or? We saved money by retaining the stock wheels, minimizing the number of parts and trinkets we purchased, and sticking with the stock paint job.

Know Where You're Going

In order to get a tight focus on the type of customizing you're trying to do and what you expect the bike to look like at the end, it's a good idea to put together a file of bikes you like. This can be pages cut out of magazines (just save the bike pictures) or snap shots from shows and travels to Sturgis, or Myrtle, or whatever.

If you're computer literate, you can even load a nice side view photo of your bike onto the hard drive and then modify it with photoshop or the program of your choice. Try a new color or (more difficult) a new set of wheels.

The blue and white Bagger is another of Brian Klock's Newstalgia machines. What started as a 2001 Heritage now looks very much like a Dresser from "1966."

The Heritage came with some of the correct components, including the sixteen inch tires and wheels on both ends. Bags are from Harley-Davidson, while the extended rear fender is a Klock Werks Special. Tru-Dual exhaust is from Samson.

PAINT

As good as the factory paint jobs are, it's hard to have a truly custom bike without a custom paint job. There are two kinds of custom paint jobs. The less expensive kind where only the sheet metal is painted, and the more expensive, and truly custom, kind that involve painting the frame as well as the sheet metal.

In the case of the former, the best part is the limited number of parts that need to be painted. At least as compared to a Bagger.

The whitewall tires, oval air cleaner, and period correct paint job all help to reinforce the mid-1960s theme. Windshield is from a current Deluxe.

The bad news is the fact that you need to stick with colors that work with the (generally) black frame. Or use graphics that contain black elements to tie everything together. As to the other more expensive kind of paint job, you are required to pull the bike all the way down to a bare frame. You're not just looking at money, you're looking at a lot of work as well.

Which brings us back to planning. Based on the other bikes you admire or lust after, decide what you would do if money were no object. Itemize each item on the Dream Bike. Now go back over the list and figure out which items have to be deleted to make the dream fit reality. Don't forget to read the Paint and Sheet Metal chapter farther along in this book.

THE INTERVIEWS

For help deciding what you should and shouldn't do to that Softail in the garage we asked our panel of experts for a little advice. We asked each one what they would do with a late model Softail and a budget of twelve thousand dollars. The budget does not include motor work and assumes the owner does most of the labor. Obviously, we're talking about projects that don't

The front end features a dropped fender with extra trim and Dakota Billet flush-mount axle.

involve any heavy fabrication work. Near the end of each interview we asked what they would do with an even smaller budget.

Some of our experts gave specific design ideas and others offered advice of a more general nature. Together, this group offers well over one hundred years of experience customizing Harley-Davidsons, so read on and take it to heart.

DONNIE SMITH

I would go to a 250 or 240 swingarm kit. That would make a big statement, it would take the bike to a new level and help it stand out in a crowd. That kit is five to six thousand dollars, so there goes a big chunk of your budget. The kit comes with a rear fender, so you might as well change the front fender too and then get a paint job. Paint makes the bike, that's three to five thousand, it depends on where you live and who you have do the work. You would have to change the seat obviously, some kits have seats or seat pans with them. And there you are, that's pretty well used up your budget. I would do it that way.

If you wanted to do something more moderate, you could buy wheels, a set of wheels and rotors is thirty-five hundred to four thousand and tires are four hundred more. If it was a Fat Boy or Heritage you could try 18 inch wheels and keep the stock fenders. You could paint the stock dash or buy one from someone like Milwaukee Iron.

From scratch-built customs like the bike in the upper photo, to redesigned Harley-Davidsons like the one below, Donnie Smith bikes all share a certain ultra clean look and incredible attention to detail.

Dan Piprude started with a 2005 Softail Custom, added all the standard items like bars, grips, and a big-bore kit, then took the bike to Donnie Smith. Donnie and crew put on the new swingarm and 240 rear tire.

19

Instead of billet wheels, Dan and Donnie elected to stay with 18 inch spoked wheels on both ends. Working the classic theme, Donnie added a new-style tombstone taillight from Kuryakyn at the rear. Dan wanted "an old school Harley, but one that still looked bad-ass."

Like Donnie Smith, all of Dave Perewitz's bikes have a certain "look." The lines are clean and all the pieces work together to create a great design.

On a Springer I like to rake the frame, they handle better that way. We add a moderate amount of additional rake, like five to seven degrees. The extra rake also levels the bike out so they aren't going uphill. That's what we did with Scott Morgan's bike (see the Gallery section). On a Springer you can't change the front wheel size, because the fender fits that 21 inch wheel, unless you throw the front fender away.

You can get into moderately wider rear tires, like a 150 instead of 130. The stock rear fender is stuffed that way so it isn't so empty and actually makes the tire look bigger than it is. You could change fenders, bob them or change them, or add a strutless fender if you find one you like. That would help give the back end another look. And there are stretched gas tanks that drop right on the stock frame.

If you change the tank or get rid of the stock dash you have to hang a speedo on the bars or whatever. Some of those have idiot lights so you wouldn't lose the oil light and all that. The ignition switch needs to be moved now, there are some motor mounts that have a provision for the ignition switch which puts them on the left side of the motor right under the tank.

DAVID PEREWITZ

Longtime customizer and custom motorcycle fabricator Dave Perewitz approached the idea of customizing a bike a little differently. David gave us his ideas for a budget bike first, and the more elaborate bike second, based partly on a very recent customizing job to come through his shop.

We recently did a bike for a charity organization, every year they give away a new Harley, but their raffle ticket sales were starting to drop off and they needed something to spruce things up. They gave me a new 2006, Fat Boy to customize. They're on a budget natural-ly, they wanted to spend between five and seven thou-sand dollars.

So my job is to give them the most impact for their money. Naturally I said we had to do new paint. But first we put on a new front fender, a Wernimont fender mounted closer to the tire. Then we smoothed off the stock rear fender and added a taillight from Russ Wernimont. It's not a bolt on taillight, you have to drill new holes, but it's a nice looking unit and it includes the directional lights. For paint we did a traditional flame job, red with flames is probably the highest impact paint job you can do. We did a lowering kit in the back, one of the ones that you add onto the stock shocks. For pipes we added some Donnie Smith pipes from Samson. The seat we put on is from Danny Gray.

The Fat Boy came with lower legs that are not chrome plated, so we swapped those for chrome legs, and added the simple bolt on stuff, like an air cleaner insert, pulley cover,

In building the raffle bike, Dave relied on cleaned-up sheet metal and bright paint rather than a plethora of chrome accessories. Photo courtesy of Laconia Rotary and Shetler Photography.

When it's right, it's right. Another Perewitz bike, one that started life as a Twin Cam Fat Boy!

In addition to the wide swingarm and fat rear tire, Dave stretched and raked the stock frame.

Here you can see the frame's new front section, and the Russ Wernimont one-piece tank.

Built for Dave King, the former Fat Boy is painted in PPG Prizmatique blue, with flames done by Dave Perewitz and Keith Hanson.

chrome levers, new mirrors and a pair of Ness grips. We left the wheels alone, but just those few modifications really made the bike stand out and gave them a different bike than any other vendor raffling off a new Harley-Davidson.

If they had wanted to spend more money, like eight to twelve thousand dollars, then I would do a lot of the same things, like changing the front fender, the pipes, rear lowering kit, Danny Gray seat and the new taillight, but I would do more. With the extra money I would stretch the gas tank, and add a one-piece dash. The other big thing would be to rake the frame to get an extra six degrees of rake. People don't realize that you can do that without taking the bike apart. And as long as we have more money we can change the handle bars, add chrome controls and maybe install chrome-plated calipers.

Dave, what are the mistakes riders make when they customize their first bike?

The biggest, biggest mistake is they don't start with a plan. They start by buying everything piece by piece, what ever they can afford this week or this month. That's the easiest way to go but it's the biggest mistake too. The really unfortunate part is they don't realize the mistake they've made 'till they are in too deep.

Guys come in to have us work on their bikes and they already have ten to fifteen thousand dollars invested in bolt-ons, and we take all that off and throw the stuff in the corner and we usually don't end up re-using much of it.

So you have to have a plan. You can't just buy parts one item at a time. It's difficult though for the average guy to focus on a bike like that. They know what they want, but don't know how to get there, and they don't have competent bike shop owners to work with either. Generally speaking, the shops just want to sell the parts and don't think about the end result.

In fact, we are thinking about offering a consulting service for guys who want help customizing their bike, even if they don't have a lot of money to spend. The problem is, let's say we charge them 500 dollars, most guys would say, 'I don't want to spend 500 bucks, I can buy parts with that money.'

What they don't realize is they would save so much money. They wouldn't buy any parts that aren't compatible or don't fit – which happens all the time and the only way you know about it is through experience. The biggest advantage would be the end result. When they're done the bike wouldn't look like just another black Fat Boy with some accessories added on.

ARLEN NESS

Let me describe the process by the things I would do first, second and so on. The first thing I always do to a bike is new wheels and brakes, an 18 in the rear and maybe a 21 in front with that new 130 Avon tire.

New pipes are always a must, that would be next. Most guys like to change the bars and maybe the seat. And depending on the model, you may want to add some chrome to the front end. Now you probably have six or seven grand in the bike. If you're going to keep going, a paint job is next. That's about three thousand depending on how far you go.

If you want a really new look for the bike, then you have to buy sheet metal. A new front and rear fender, and extend the gas tank, that's probably easy a thousand bucks, of course now you have to do the paint job. You might want to do a tail dragger fender for both front and rear

Or maybe digger fenders front and rear, they're all

It's one thing to build a cool bike, or five cool bikes. It's something altogether different to stay on top of the custom motorcycle industry for well over thirty years, all the while helping other riders build some very nifty bikes of their own. Jeff McMillan, courtesy of Arlen Ness Motorcycles

Being a great designer means having the balls to try something totally new - like this turbine powered motorcycle based on a helicopter engine wrapped in Bob Monroe built body panels. Jeff McMillan, courtesy of Arlen Ness Motorcycles

Perhaps Arlen's greatest gift is his ability to think outside the box, and still be able to help individuals build simple clean Softails and Baggers. Jeff McMillan, courtesy of Arlen Ness Motorcycles

If you take the time to read Paul's interview, you'll find he has some very interesting ideas regarding color and texture. PYO

about the same amount of money. It depends on the look you like. You could turn a Softail into a chopper pretty easy with a tail dragger rear fender and high bars. It's a matter of which style you like.

The other route would be the high performance look with one of the 300 rear tire kits. They come with a swingarm, rear wheel and a rear fender, and you should buy a matching front wheel. Those are big money though, six or seven thousand dollars. In a way you get less for your money, because the wheel kit is so expensive. If you have any money left over you can buy all the little things like mirrors, grips and pegs.

Arlen, what are the mistakes people make when they start customizing their bike.

The first-time guys always spend a lot of money at the dealership on their new bike. And it's all what I call "me too" stuff. Chrome trinkets and that kind of thing. You can spend a lot of money that way. And then when they go to their first event they see that half the bikes there have exactly the same accessories that they do. They get a lot more for the money if they look in the magazines and really figure out what they want before they spend a lot of money on accessories. They need to do some research and have a good idea what they want before they start. Then they can come to a shop like ours or, any good shop, for help picking out and ordering the right parts that will get them that look they want.

PAUL YAFFE

Let's say it's a Softail Custom. The first thing to do is decide what you want for the overall look of the bike. Do you want it long and low, or a bobber, or what? And how will you use the bike, what is your riding style? Do you want to profile around town or do long distance travel? Usage is critical so you get what you want in the end.

The profile of the bike that you create with the sheet metal is the biggest statement the bike will make. You want them to look at the bike and think, "wow, that's different," or "hey, that's really cool." Personally, I would most likely do a long and low bike, that's where my tastes lie. I would cut the frame, depending on the size of the person riding the bike, pull it 5 inches forward with 40 degrees of rake.

We had a guy come to us with a Fat Boy, Dave Veres from the Chicago Cubs. He wanted something that looked like one of my bikes, but he already had a lot of money invested in the Fat Boy. So rather than sell it and start over, I took his bike and raked it and stretched it five inches with a new front frame section, added one of our stretched tanks, and new rear fender, and it came out great. I tried to customize the bike but make sure it was still usable on a daily basis. There's nothing worse than having a bike you don't like. It's nice to profile, but its better to ride. The geometry of the front end is important so the bike handles good. And your arms and feet have to end up in the right place, you want to be comfortable and able to reach the controls. What he spent for his bike went past the twelve thousand dollar budget, but those are the kinds of bikes I like.

More than just a really cool aftermarket Softail, Paul's Discovery bike is a very interesting design, one with a lot of motion, even while standing still. PYO

Another aftermarket Softail from Paul Yaffe, one with the long neck and raked fork he describes in the Q&A. PYO

What if you didn't have that much money to spend, then what would you do as a budget customizing project.

I would strip everything I could off. No turn signals, I would probably change the stock bars for apes, or drag bars, or whatever depending on the style of bike and the size of the rider. After the bars I would add new exhaust, an air cleaner, a new seat. Change the mirrors for sure. I might change the stock rear fender with a different taillight, or a side-mount light and license bracket.

And I would replace the wheels. Spoked wheels are OK if you're building a nostalgic bike, otherwise I would want to replace the stockers. They eat up a lot of the budget though, a set of wheels with matching rotors and a pulley sell for 3500 bucks.

What is the biggest mistake people make when they start out to customize a bike.

The biggest mistake is all that bolt-on stuff people get when they first buy a new bike. Chrome covers and trinkets and all that. Then six months later they see other more radical bikes and then they want to do something else. Once they're edu-cated they want to do more than just bolt-on stuff, but they have so much money tied up in all those chrome accessories.

I tell people to leave it stock for awhile, maybe just upgrade the motor. Spend the time getting to know the motorcycle and looking at other bikes. Then decide what to do. Think carefully about paint. Bright paint might be OK now but you'll be sick of it in six months. With stock bikes, when I customize them, I often use factory colors or factory racing colors.

I like metallics, silvers and grays, muted colors. I'm not big on bright purple with neon. Why not celebrate the fact that it is a Harley-Davidson? Like the Softail I had in Sturgis this year (in our Gallery section), the dominant colors on that bike are orange and black. It came with the bead blasted and silver motor. I brought silver into the paint job so it makes it look like the silver motor is what I wanted. I tried to make use of the textures that are already there. It's OK to get away from chrome, The exhaust on that bike is flat black with gloss black heat shields.

If you've got a bike with some bead blasted parts, bead blast more stuff to make it look like that is what you want to do. Make it custom without doing what everybody else does. Mix textures. Try something new rather than just chrome plating every-thing.

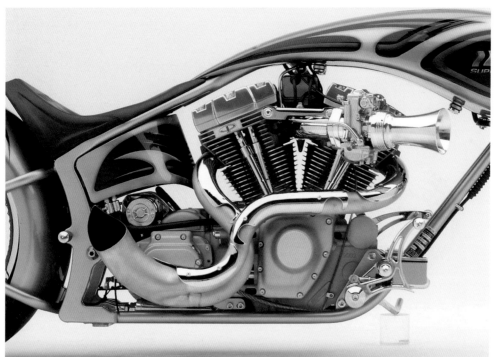

The PYO Phantom pipes are a good example of Paul's advice to mix textures and not rely on chrome plate for everything. PYO

Project Softail - The Bobber

Making a Bobber out of a late model Softail seemed the ideal project for the Softail book. After all, Bobbers are popular right now and *all* we had to do was install a new short rear fender, throw away the front fender, install a solo seat and get rid of the factory dash (maybe). We started the mock up with a 2002 Night Train, though the Night Train would be replaced later by a Softail Standard.

What you see here is the first planning and mock up session. And we can't emphasize enough the importance of the mock up for any kind of customizing project. As explained, the Night Train was replaced with a Standard, but both are late-model bikes and the chassis and swingarm are the same so it really isn't a big deal. Just follow along as we try to decide which fender best fits our "keep it simple" Bobber project.

Disassembly

The disassembly is straightforward, the only real trick is to disconnect the wiring, which must be done before the fender and rails can be removed. Most late model Harleys route the rear turn signal wires into the taillight housing. This makes more sense if you take off the taillight lens and scrutinize the way the wires from the blinkers are routed up into the housing and then turn and plug into the light-base.

Once we had the bike apart, Neil and Ken tried three different fenders before finding one that seemed to hold promise. We tried a late model front Dresser fender, a round fender blank, and a re-pop of an early Springer fender meant for 1937 to 1948 models. I was trying for a late-Bobber/early Chopper look and the front Springer fender, stripped of its supporting brackets and turned around, seemed the best fit, both literally and aesthetically.

The photos tell the story of our little planning or mock-up session better than words. In the end we had to cut the bottom off the fender, then do a pie cut to ensure the fender would follow the radius of the wheel. The work on the fender picks up again in Chapter Three.

After disconnecting the wires inside the taillight housing, and taking off the outer struts, you can get down to business.

Once the fender is out of the way the inner fender comes off next. This will be used again.

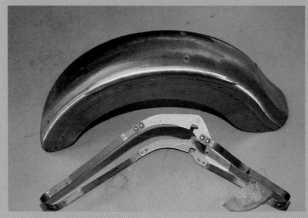

We tried a variety of fenders and settled on this early Springer fender. Before proceeding we had to cut the supports out of the old fender

It took a series of trial fittings before the fender started to show promise as our Bobber fender. We've taken the belt guards off the other side.

Here you can see the new, shorter fender.

The bottom needs to be cut off. After marking the length with a market, Ken wraps the fender with paper and runs the marker along the paper's edge.

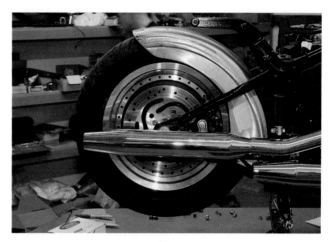

You can do a lot with paper templates, here we've essentially changed the radius of the fender with a piece of light board.

A zinger and cut-off wheel are used to do the cutting.

We make a bigger template, slice it in two places and then determine how much the inside slit overlaps to make the board match our ideal radius.

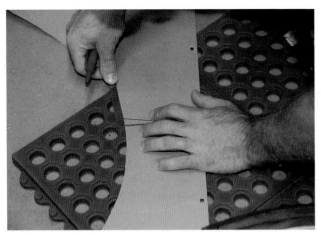

The shape of the overlapping triangle determines the size of the pie-cut that needs to be made.

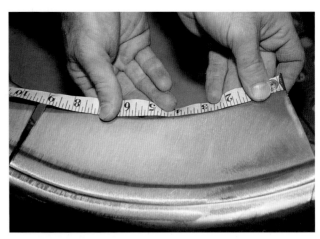

...measures the distance and then transfers the measurement to the other side so the two cuts are in exactly the same place.

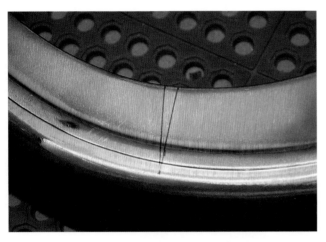

Here's the pie-cut marked out on the fender.

Once the two wedges are cut out of the fender, you can see how the radius tightens up.

Ken cuts out the wedge of metal...

After tack welding the fender at the pie-cuts we do another trial fitting. Life is good as the inside radius is a good match for the wheel.

Chapter Three

Sheet Metal & Paint

Make the Profile Your Own

When you truly customize a bike you change the sheet metal, all in an attempt to change the profile. Your particular choice of sheet metal will depend on the plan. Is this going to be a Bobber or Chopper, or just a clean, simple custom. For the purposes of this book we've decided to stay with a mild-custom theme. Most of the bikes are not radical re-designs and only a few have any changes to the frame's rake and stretch. The ideas that follow are just that, ideas. Each intended to help you create a motorcycle you

Built at the Klock Werks shop, this Evo powered Softail uses a Twin Cam swingarm and belt to get a 180 tire tucked under the Klock Werks rear fender.

can call your very own. There are two fender mounting sequences farther along in the chapter, one done on our Project Softail.

Because your Softail is one of the most popular motorcycles of all time, there is no shortage of parts designed to fit that frame. From front fenders to stretched tanks and tail dragger rear fenders, if you don't find what you want you aren't looking hard enough. There are even some interesting mix-and-match options using Harley-Davidson parts.

Once the sheet metal is chosen and mocked up, it's time for paint. We've covered paint in a general sense at the end of this chapter, including the work done on our project Softail. We've also included some ideas for "paint jobs" that are really just airbrush and/or pinstripe work. Which means you don't have to strip off the paint and may not even have to take the sheet metal off the bike.

FRONT FENDERS

As stated by Arlen Ness and Paul Yaffe in Chapter Two, the first thing you have to do is decide on the look you're after, the profile. Now match the fender choices to that look. Both fenders you choose should match the look you're trying to achieve.

The front fender is by far the easiest to change. Having said that, most fenders come raw, meaning they are not drilled for the mounting bolts. Which means you have to mock up the fender on the bike, determine the exact position and then drill the holes. From Russ Wernimont to Arlen Ness, the fenders come as blanks, some assembly required.

There are a few exceptions. Drag Specialties has a line of fenders predrilled, just add paint. And there are the factory fenders, which come with the holes already drilled. In some cases you can even

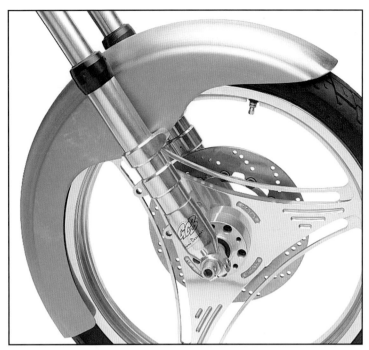

Available through Drag Specialties, The Duster from Russ Wernimont (RWD) is designed for either 19 or 21 inch front wheels. RWD

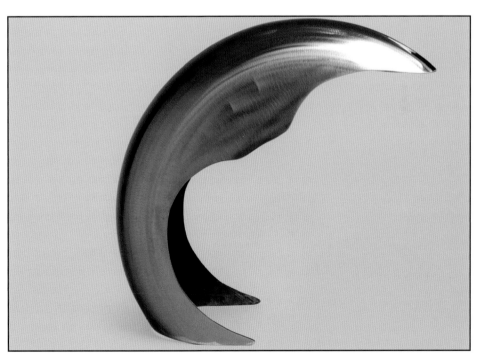

Paul Yaffe (PYO) offers this long front fender, the DEI, meant as an upgrade for a Heritage or Fat Boy. Works well over a 16 or 18 inch wheel with low profile tire. PYO

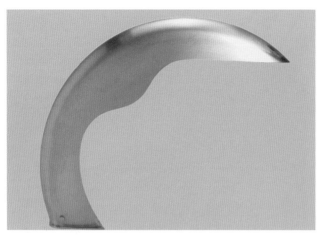

The Front Dragger from Arlen Ness is designed to work with a Tail Dragger in back, fits 16, 17 and 18 inch tires, available in two widths. Ness

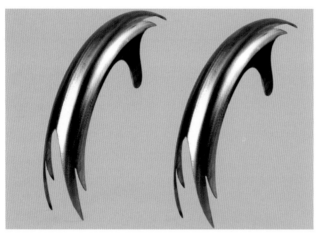

These "wild" front fenders could only have come from Paul Yaffe. Bolt them to the radical ride of your choice. PYO

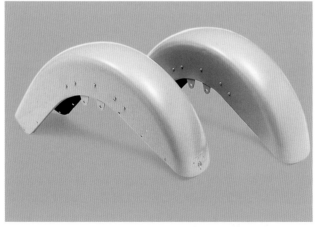

If you want to create your own Heritage, or classic Softail, these "Heritage" fenders are available with, or without, holes for trim. Biker's Choice

buy these high-quality fenders already painted to match the rest of your bike.

If you want a truly custom bike however, you're going to want a custom fender. One that comes in raw steel, or fiberglass and requires you go through the whole mock-up and paint process.

REAR FENDERS

More work than the front, a new rear fender can really change the look of your Softail and help separate it from all the other Softails parked outside the Broken Spoke. A trim fender can define your bike as a Bobber, while a long tail dragger will lower the bike and help it look like a sophisticated custom. Stock Softails suffer from fender and strut designs that have changed very little during the bike's lifetime. The stock chrome "angle iron" fender strut doesn't follow the line of the fender, and holds the fender so far up off the tire that some of the bikes "look like dirt bikes" to quote Arlen Ness.

So even though it generally requires cutting the stock fender struts and may look like too much work, there's much to be gained by replacing the stock rear sheet metal. First, you get rid of the kink in the stock fender strut and may get rid of the strut altogether. Second, you lower the fender on the bike, which pulls the whole machine closer to the ground. Finally, and perhaps most important, you've gone a long way toward establishing your own profile.

Pick a design that compliments the rest of the design for your bike and follow the easy steps outlined farther along to make that new fender part of the new machine. And if your mechanical skills are limited, you can always pay the local customizing shop to cut the struts and mock-up the new fender. Just be sure you're there for the mock-up session, because even a small change in the position of a fender can have a huge impact on the looks of the bike.

Don't forget that the wires to the taillight and signals have to (unless it's a side-mount light) run inside the fender. Some fenders have tabs or tubing in the corner to hold the wiring away from the tire. Or you can weld a piece of tubing up into the corner of the fender. You could even use something like JB Weld to glue the tubing in place. As always, be sure the tire can't hit the tubing or the little metal tabs.

THE MOCK-UP

Unless it's a fender that's predrilled for your particular bike, you can't just bolt the new fender, front or rear, to the bike. You have to take off the old one and patiently decide exactly where and how to mount the new one. We've said it before but it bears repeating: the position and angle of the fender is critical to the way the bike looks. Take your time during the mock-up process. Be sure you can step back from the bike to get a true view of the machine, something you can't do when the garage is so small you've got your nose pressed up against the sheet metal. Try to get the bike at ride height, not held in an unnatural position with a jack for example, when you make the visual judgments.

In general the inside radius of the fender should match the radius of the rim, which is why a fender designed for a sixteen inch tire often looks somehow wrong when used on an eighteen inch wheel and tire. In the case of Project Softail, the fender we used had to be pie-cut so the inside radius would match the radius of the rim, and even then it's not a perfect match. We used pieces of gas line taped up inside the fender to hold it up off the tire during the process. Professional shops often use a broken 1-1/2 inch drive belt, taped to the tire, to hold the fender up off the tire. Obviously you can use anything of the right dimension, thought the drive belt has the advantage of being flat so the new fender tends to sit right where you want it without cocking to one side.

MOUNTING FENDERS

Obviously the fender you choose needs to be the right width for the fork spacing, or the width of the fender struts. Mounting needs to be done carefully so that the fender and hardware can't touch the tire, won't shake loose, and provides the fender with enough support that it won't crack later.

The actual bolting should be done with Nylock type nuts, which have the advantage of locking without being super-tight, a nice feature when you're mounting 'glass or plastic fenders. As mentioned elsewhere, use button-head Allens and aim the bolt away from the tire or at least cut the bolt so there are no extra threads sticking out past the end of the nut to snag on the tire. The clearance between the fender, mounting hardware and the tire should be checked through the full range of suspension travel. Consider that tires often more slightly past the "end

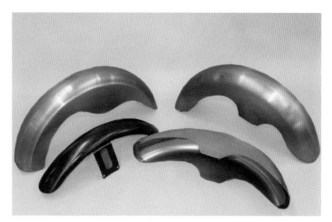

We borrowed this sequence from a scratch-building project, just to illustrate the importance of the mock up. Above are the 4 fenders we bought or borrowed before trying to decide which one best fit the design.

Long or short, that's the question, and what kind of bars best fit the bike as well. You have to be able to step back from the bike...

... to accurately judge the effect of different sheet metal choices. You might even have to roll the bike outside.

33

Same project seen on page 33. After choosing a fender and having the sheet metal painted we had to mount it. Black tubing holds fender up off the tire.

If we weren't using a spacer, we could make a template with the shape of the boss on the lower leg and use that as our guide.

Of course the holes should have been drilled before paint. We use the fender spacers as a template, in this shot the spacers are held in place with cut-off bolts...

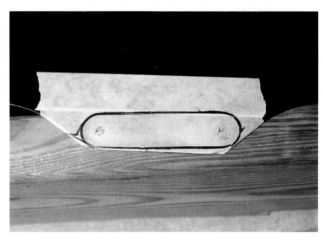

After marking the outline of the spacer and center-punching the location of the holes it's time for drilling.

...screwed into the lower legs. Once we're real sure of the fender position we clamp the fender (gently) in place and mark location of the spacer.

This is a stepped drill bit, better suited to sheet metal work than a standard fluted drill.

of travel" when you hit a big bump. Especially if your svelte sweetie is on the passenger pillion.

Finally, everybody wants the fender close to the tire. Especially in the case of the front fender, it's tempting to put the fender so close to the tire that it almost touches the rubber. It looks so damned cool. The first problem however, comes if the fender shifts even a little. The second and more common problem comes when you wind it up to 80 miles per hour on the first highway trip. Tires, especially street tires, grow at speed. At best the friction creates heat which burns the paint off the fender, at worst, the tire stops turning or tears the fender off its mounts.

CUTTING TEMPLATES

Installing a new front fender often means cutting a template and then drilling the actual hole with a stepped drill rather than a conventional fluted drill. For more on the use or templates see our little how-to sequence nearby.

GAS TANKS

Most of us are going to leave the gas tank alone, though there are a number of easy options here. For the pre-2000 Softails extension kits for the stock Fat Bob tanks, and tanks with the extensions already in place, are available from a number of catalogs. For the 2000 and later bikes extension kits don't show up in the current catalogs, though it might be we just aren't looking hard enough. Complete tanks with a two inch extension, ready to drop onto your tank (after paint), are available for both carbureted and fuel injected bikes. There are also a number of smooth top tanks from companies like Russ Wernimont Design and available through Drag Specialties, that will bolt right on the stock late model Softail frame, though you're going to have to relocate the ignition switch, speedo and warning lights.

Any fabrication shop should be able to add a two inch extension to a stock tank, though we should note that welding on the thin steel that makes up a factory gas tank requires skill. Not only is the metal thin, it's under a certain amount of tension. Caved in tank tops can result from too much heat. As long as we're talking about welding, anyone who adds mounting tabs to a custom tank needs to have enough skill that the bracket or tank doesn't crack later.

A classic in its own right, the Legacy from Arlen Ness works well on a Heritage. Available in different widths, the Legacy is 4 inches longer than stock. Ness

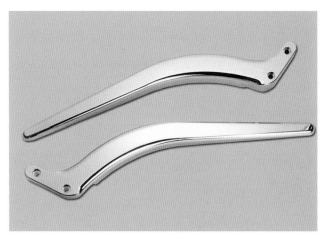

Replace those kinked fender struts on that stock Softail with these billet struts from Arlen. Lower the fender on the bike at the same time. Ness

The Maverick from Russ Wernimont comes in three widths, up to 9 inches wide. RWD

The Show Me is another Paul Yaffe rear fender design and comes raw with no mounting holes or internal struts. PYO

Weld on (and some glue on) tank extension kits are available for most of the standard factory tanks. Biker's Choice

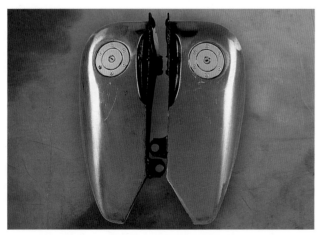

Or, for owners of pre-2000 Softails, you can buy tanks with two inch extensions already welded in place, ready for primer and paint. Drag Specialties.

PAINT

As mentioned by more than one of our interview experts in Chapter Two, there is nothing that will set your bike apart from all the others like a custom paint job. All the chrome trim and lowered shocks in the world won't make your bike stand apart from all the other Softails like a nice custom paint job.

In the case of Project Softail, we decided to stay with the black theme, as given us by Harley-Davidson (see the painting sequence in this chapter). When it comes to paint, you need to bring your checkbook because it ain't cheap. We chose black because it was easy and saved us money, and it worked with our basic Bobber/Chopper theme.

A true custom paint job includes the frame. Which means a complete tear down. Most of us aren't building true custom bikes here, and don't want to pull a late-model bike down to the bare frame. When you decide to retain the black frame the paint job you choose needs to be something that will work with that frame. Note Paul Yaffe's comments regarding this topic in Chapter Two.

WHERE TO GET IDEAS AND HELP

Ideas for a paint job are as close as your local magazine rack. Each town of any size has at least one paint shop that specializes in motorcycles. People are quick to praise a painter and even quicker to bitch about jobs gone sour. Find out who does the best work and then stop by to look at their portfolio or scrap book. Discuss prices. The good painters are true artists, it doesn't hurt to ask them for ideas.

If it's an elaborate paint job you have to find a painter you trust, you can't be there for every step and he or she will have to interpret your original idea. This isn't a bad thing. A good painter can often expand on your idea or an idea from a magazine to create something far better than the original concept.

Before deciding on a paint job think about your goals for the bike, your own tastes and your plans for the bike. Styles come and go. The heavy graphics look seems to be gone for now. Flames tend to be timeless though they may run their course as well. Currently there seems to be a lot of flame jobs that are morphing into tribal designs. An elaborate paint job sets your bike apart like nothing else. The downside is the cost and the extra work of disassembly.

The non-paint paint job

You don't have to pull the sheet metal off your bike, have it sanded and stripped, and then painted and clearcoated. Instead you can have the existing paint job enhanced with airbrushed images and/or pinstripes.

Every major and minor event, from Sturgis to your own local bike show, has airbrush vendors willing to add images to your existing paint job. Though it's hard to get the same visual impact from airbrushing you get from a complete paint job, you can do it all in one afternoon for a lot less than a complete paint job.

Some of the airbrushing falls into the "quaint" or "trite" category. Think twice about flags and flowers and go for something that compliments your existing paint while at the same time adding to the overall look you're trying to achieve. Pinstripes can be used here as well and often work well with the factory paint. Done in an early style, extensive pinstripes can help to give the bike an old-skool look appropriate for a Bobber or Chopper.

The H-D Color Shop

The factory began offering custom paint some time ago and each year the program gets better and better. If you don't have one, get a new Accessories catalog and look through the Color Shop section. If nothing else, it's filled with good painting ideas. Consider that you're buying the sheet metal as well as the paint. Which means you can sell the old sheet metal on eBay, or the local swap meet, or save it to make your bike a convertible.

The nice thing about the factory's paint program is the fact that you know ahead of time what you're getting and you know the quality is top-shelf. Harley also makes seats to match many of these paint jobs, which adds a nice finishing touch to the paint job.

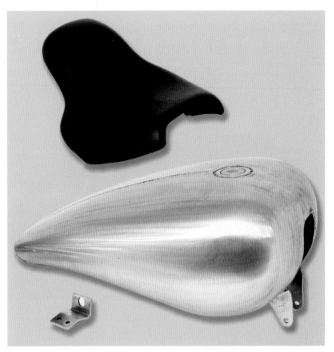

If you're trying to achieve a new profile but don't want to cut the frame, try this kit from Paul Yaffe. Includes an already-stretched tank designed to drop onto a stock 2000 and up frame, and matching solo seat. Bracket makes ignition switch relocation easy. Comes with ideas for relocated speedo. PYO

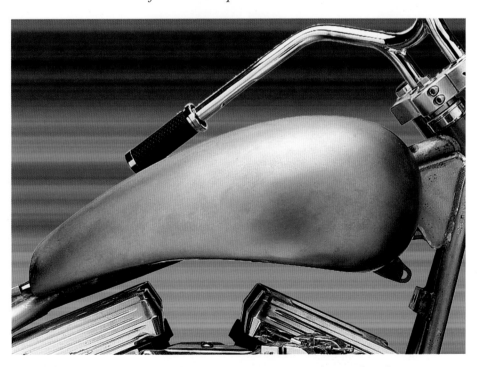

This one-piece custom tank from Russ Wernimont is designed to drop onto stock 2000 and later Softail frames, "but requires the relocation of ignition switch, speedo etc." RWD

Project Softail - The Bobber

1. It's a long story why, but we changed the Project bike to the 2005 Standard shown here.

2. The fender we trimmed and pie-cut earlier fits pretty well (the swingarms are the same).

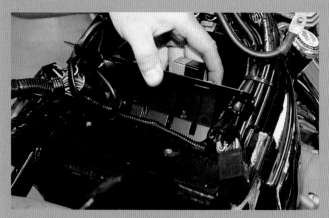

4. Positioning the module behind the battery means pushing this fuse and relay assembly farther down in the cavity behind the battery.

Our Softail Project, last seen at American Thunder, made its way to the Dougz shop in La Crosse, Wisconsin. That is, the fender and a brand new 2005 Softail Standard, made their way to Dougz. And as the photos show, the project started up again about where it left off at American Thunder.

First Doug and Terry had to strip off all the stock sheet metal and then get a feel for the new fender, how would it fit and mount to the swingarm. As the swingarms themselves are all the same between the 2002 Night Train and the 2005 Standard, there were no major hiccups in the initial part of the project at Dougz.

Possibly the hardest part of this whole project was deciding what to do with the ignition module. Unlike an Evo, which can be converted to a system contained entirely under the points cover, the Twin Cam engines use a large box that houses the brains for the ignition system. Normally this box resides in a concave fender insert under the seat. As our Bobber would use a fender mounted to the swingarm and

3. The BIG issue becomes: what to do with the ignition module. Evo owners have it easy.

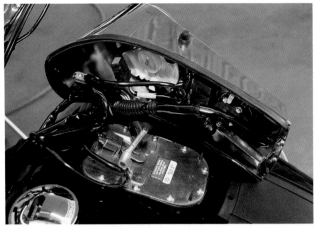

Doug disconnects everything under the dash and the gas gauge/fuel pump wires, then only two bolts hold the tank on the frame.

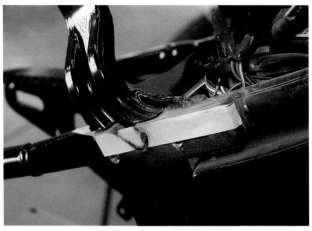

Cutting the strut off is hard, partly because just behind it is the cross brace welded in at an angle that tips it uphill toward the back of the bike.

We want to achieve that true Hardtail line that runs straight from the neck to the rear axle. Doug marks out the line with a piece of masking tape.

So Doug cuts the area behind the strut with a plasma cutter, in two steps. Here you see him doing the initial cutting just behind the strut.

This is the do-or-die moment. Doug begins cutting the frame struts off with a zinger and cut off wheel.

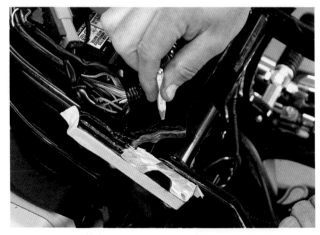

To clean things up, and maintain "the line," Doug marks the cross brace before cutting off another small piece with the plasma cutter.

The finished cutting, prior to a little clean up.

Now it's easier to truly judge the effect of the new fender, without the struts sticking up in the air.

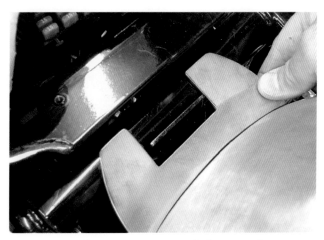

Doug manufactures a very simple brace as shown...

placed farther back than a stock fender, there was no way to mount the module to the new fender.

The harness going into the module looks like the main harness for the Space Shuttle, or a least the main harness for a Cadillac. There are a lot of wires, cutting them in order to splice in longer wires and thus make it easy to move the module didn't seem like a good idea. After considering all our options Doug suggested mounting the module on the cross-bar just behind the battery as shown in the photos. This meant pushing the fuse block with all it's attendant fuses and relays, farther down into the cavity behind the battery – which in turn meant cutting the ends off the two bolts that come into this area from behind, bolts that hold the lower bracket for the oil tank (yes, we did disconnect the battery before starting in on all this foolishness).

GAS TANK

Once we have a home for the module, Doug takes the gas tank off, which means disconnecting the line at the bottom of our fuel injected bike. This is done by sliding the collar on the fitting up and then pulling the line off the fitting. The cross-over tube comes off too, after siphoning most of the fuel out of the tank. There's also a vent line at the front of the tank. The speedo and ignition switch wires simply disconnect from the fuel pump base on the bottom of the dash, after the dash is unbolted and tipped up off the tank.

CUT, CUT, CUT

With the tank off the bike it's easy to envision the line we want the frame to have in the area of the struts. Doug marks this line with a piece of tape and goes to town with a zinger. Unfortunately, the cross-bar located behind the struts is tipped up toward the back, which will foil our plan to have a nice straight line running from the neck all the way down the frame and onto the swingarm – like a true hardtail. So after cutting nearly all the way through the strut, Doug cuts the area inside where the strut meets the cross-bar with a plasma cutter. And after the struts are out of the way he cuts this area back even farther (this all makes more sense if you check out the photos).

Now we do another mock-up session with the struts gone. The bike is finally starting to look like a proper Bobber. The goal here is to have a bike reminiscent of the late Bobber/early Choppers from the

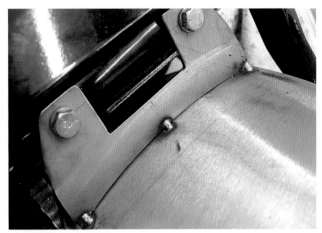

... that will be tack welded to the fender and drilled. The bolts screw into holes that are drilled and tapped into the cross brace for the swingarm.

Doug's guiding philosophy in finishing the fender was, "how would a guy at home do this in the 1960s."

The concave panel shown will reinforce the left side of the fender and still allow clearance for the belt.

Round stock was deemed stronger than flat stock for the supports at the back of the fender.

After welding the seam and cleaning it up with a small grinder the patch needs only a little filler and some primer.

The bottom tabs, on the right, are cut with a radius that matches the big outer washers used on the stock Softail.

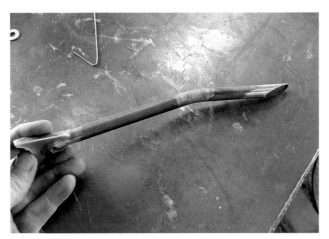

This is the finished strut, before being welded to the upper fender tab.

Close up shows how the tab will bolt to the fender.

Another mock up, things are falling into place.

The raw strut, ready to be welded to the big axle washer.

era before Choppers turned into long radical rides with super long forks and extreme rake angles. In keeping with that theme Doug fabricates simple mounting brackets for the fender, as a guy working in his own garage might have in the 1960s.

Once the fender is sitting correctly on the bike, held in place with two lower bolts and the rubber tubing taped up into the inside of the fender, Doug fabricates a simple bracket between the fender and the swingarm's cross-bar. After tack welding the bracket to the fender, he drills two holes in the bracket and then drills and taps two matching holes in the cross-bar.

What's left are the rear support bars, made from round-stock bent just a bit and then welded to the big heavy washers on the outside of the swingarm, and two small fabricated tabs on the upper end. At the same time Doug forms a simple little concave piece of sheet metal to fit the spot where we cut the fender to clear the belt.

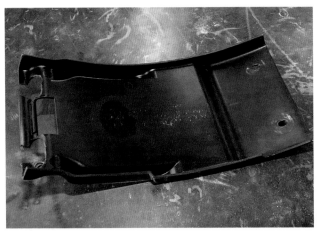

Doug decides the inner fender must be trimmed and retained, to hide and protect the electronic components located behind the oil tank.

But first Doug sands the fender with 320 grit on a small sanding block. The idea is to sand off all the guide coat so Doug knows...

After welding up the big holes and applying a little filler, Brandon applies multiple coats of primer, followed by a light "guide coat."

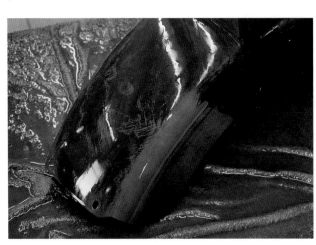

... there are no remaining low spots.

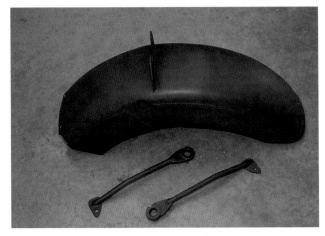

Progress shot shows the new rear fender and rear support brackets almost ready for final paint.

The tank was simply scuffed and will be painted over the factory paint.

The finished tank, as Doug and Terry decide whether or not they like the early logo.

No taillight yet, but the fender is in place and the module is bolted to the cross brace.

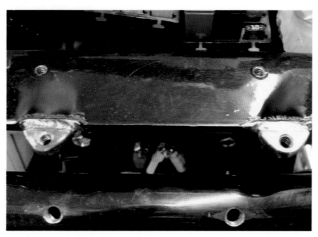

To actually mount the module to the cross brace, Doug welds on the two small tabs seen here.

Looking good, all we need now is a seat, and some black rims, and a lowering kit.

Details, first Doug needs to drill a hole for taillight wires, then add a grommet, and finally a tube to route the wires and keep them away from the tire.

Kevin Lehan from Lemans is our man with a seat. We start with the base for a solo seat but decide it's too small.

44

PREP AND PAINT

With the welder still idling in the corner, Doug fills the small holes in the fender and fills in the small kink where we did the pie-cut earlier (and hidden by the upper part of the swingarm). Metal finishing is first, done with a small grinder. Next, Doug uses a little filler on the roughest areas, followed by more sanding (much of it by hand) and then multiple coats of fast-build primer. The last coat of "primer" is a guide coat, a coat of paint lighter than the rest of the primer. This way when the fender is block sanded any remaining light paint will indicate a low spot.

The tank is scuffed at the same time, as we simply can't live with the very modern Harley-Davidson logo on our old Bobber. Some late-model logos are actually decals that are then buried under clearcoats. In that case it's necessary to grind off the decal, seal the raw metal, prime and paint. In our case, the logos are painted on at the factory, so Doug and Brandon simply scuff, seal and paint the tank. The black used on both the fender and tank is black basecoat, BC 25, from House of Kolor.

We planned at one time to hand letter the words Harley-Davidson, as that was often done, "back in the day." In the end we used original logos, as shown. These go on in a two-step process, and require no drilling so they can be put on after the tank is painted.

Once the logos are glued and screwed to the tank and the ignition switch is relocated with a Klock Werks bracket, the bike makes another journey. Kevin Lehan is in charge at the Lemans upholstery shop where they make seats for Drag Specialties. Kevin agrees to knock out a solo seat in record time as a favor (they don't do retail work at the shop).

As the photos show, we started with a very small solo seat stamped out of metal. Rather than make a larger base from vacuum-formed plastic,(which might not be strong enough) Kevin and crew flattened the solo base and added metal to the edge. Kevin designed the seat with both skirting and fringe to hide the electronics hiding under the seat.

Because of the module under the seat there really wasn't room for coil springs, and we used hairpin style springs instead. All that's left is one more trip to American Thunder.

So Kevin flattens it out and then adds almost two inches of additional material around the perimeter. Dash is removed, replaced by a leather strip that hides base for the fuel pump and looks period correct.

Kevin with his masterpiece. The fringe, and skirting underneath, hide the electronics. We used hairpin springs instead of standard coil seat springs.

Almost there and looking a lot better than just a few days earlier.

Chapter Four

Wheels, Tires, Brakes

Essential Components

After paint, wheels and tires are the most important styling items on your bike. They have an enormous effect on the bike's looks, not to mention the performance and handling. Put a fat tire kit complete with 250 or larger tire, and billet rim, on the back of your Softail and you've made a huge difference in the bike. In both a visual and functional sense, the importance of the wheels and tires simply can't be overstated.

This is what happens to an otherwise stock Softail when you add a 250 wide tire kit. This particular example converts the bike to right side drive for better overall balance. Kit includes everything but the paint and your labor. American Thunder

WHEEL TYPES

What are often called "billet" wheels are actually two or three different types of aluminum wheels. True billet wheels are carved from a solid chunk of aluminum. Most billet wheels are manufactured from 6061 T6, the first four digits identify the alloy while the T6 number refers to the heat treating specification.

Cast is the other major type of aluminum wheel. The alloy in this case is generally 356 aluminum. The expense of buying forged billets of aluminum is eliminated through casting, though tooling costs are considerable. Most cast wheels have a rim that is an integral part of the assembly, not a separate piece bolted or welded to the spokes. Because there may be some porosity in the cast material, chrome plating is more difficult with a cast wheel. Cast wheels also tend to be heavier than "billet" wheels.

At one time the billet wheels used spokes (or a center section) cut from forged aluminum, bolted or welded to a separate rim assembly. Currently, however, there are at least two methods of manufacturing a true billet wheel with an integral rim (be sure to check out the manufacturing side-bar on page 54).

TIRES

Some Softails, like the Heritage and Deluxe, come with sixteen inch tires on either end. Others like our project bike, a Standard, come with the more chop-

Just when you thought the custom wheel manufacturers couldn't come up with any really new designs, PM introduced their Contour line of custom wheels with spokes that merge with the rim itself. PM

Like most of the bigger wheel companies, PM makes rotors and pulleys that perfectly match their wheel designs. PM

Softails built before 2000, and many aftermarket wheels, come with tapered bearings, which use the central spacer as shown and shims (not shown) to set the end play per the instructions in the service manual. Biker's Choice

What you choose for tires will depend on your rim size and how you intend to use the bike. Sidewall information includes ratings for both load and speed. Some tire sizes, 18 inches for example, offer a much wider choice than others. Biker's Choice

per-esque sixteen and twenty one inch combinations.

Whether you stay with the stock sizes or change them, and what you change them to, all depend on your master plan for the bike. Don't take this too lightly. As we said, the wheels are a major part of your motorcycle. Their size and style should be used to lock in the theme or look you're trying to establish.

BRAKES

Deciding whether or not to upgrade the brakes on your Softail depends in part on how you use the bike, your overall design, your budget and whether or not you already spent big bucks for a set of wheels with matching rotors and pulley.

We have to mention the fact that earlier Softails with single piston calipers simply don't stop as well as those equipped with the newer four-piston designs used since 2000. If you have the old calipers, replace them with something better, either from H-D or the aftermarket, especially on the front end. The four-piston Harley calipers are available in chrome plate. Or you can use one of the many styles of inserts available from both H-D and the aftermarket to add a little character to the brake calipers. In spite of the very good brakes found on all late model Softails, "better" units are available from the after-

48

market. These are often superior in their engineering, though for most riders the primary advantage is increased sex appeal and aesthetics.

THE BASICS

Brakes are heat machines. A way of converting moving or kinetic energy to heat energy (remember, you can't create or destroy energy, only convert it from one form to another). More physics: a bike traveling 60 miles per hour has four times (not two) the kinetic energy of the same machine at 30 miles per hour. Though you have brakes at both ends of the motorcycle, the front brake(s) do at least 70% of the stopping on a hard brake application. So even if the trick new bike is a chopper, don't throw away that front caliper.

When it comes to picking brakes, more is usually better. More caliper pistons and more rotor surface. On a functional basis, it's hard to have too much brakes. More braking capacity means it's easier to modulate the brakes, or control them at maximum stopping pressure without any danger of lockup.

Some of the aftermarket manufacturers (PM and RC to name two) have gone to differential-bore calipers. The two or three pistons on either side or

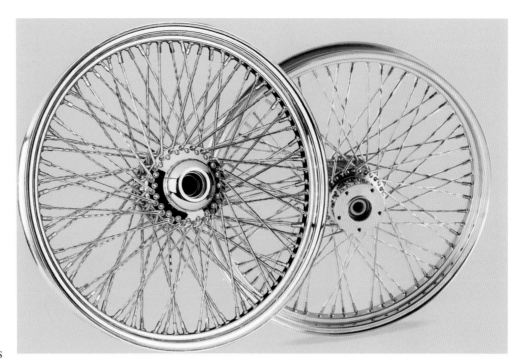

Spoked wheels often lend a classic look to a custom bike and can be purchased with straight or twisted spokes, numbering 40, 80 or more. Biker's Choice

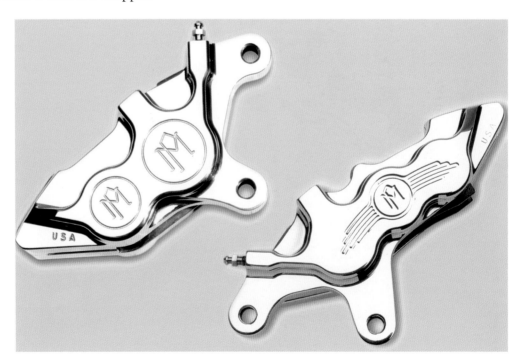

Spend the most money on the front brakes, they do most of the stopping and are more visible as well. Both the differential 4-piston design on the left, or the 6 piston caliper on the right represent very, very good braking options. PM

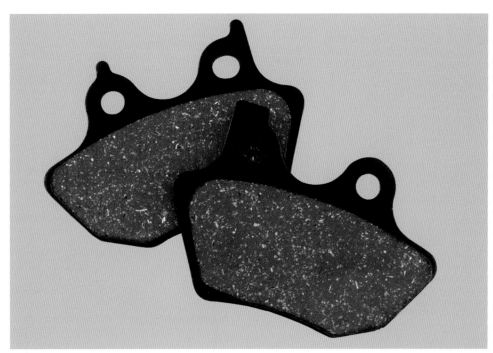

Brake pads come in a variety of flavors, and should be matched to the rotor material. Biker's Choice

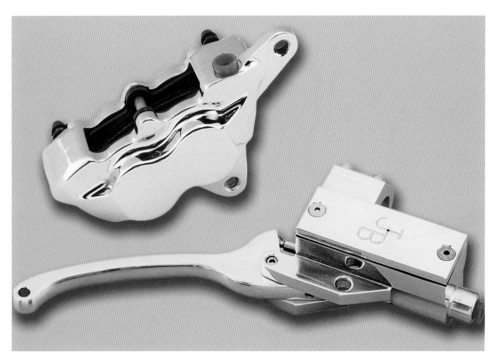

If you start replacing brake components, be sure to match the diameter of the master cylinder with the size and number of caliper pistons it's connected to. Biker's Choice

the caliper are different sizes. Normally the front edge of the rotor gets hotter than the back. To compensate for this the aftermarket manufacturers produce calipers with a leading piston that's a little bit smaller, which reduces the pressure on the leading edge slightly and evens out the pad temperature.

We also have to discuss hydraulic laws. The output, both pressure and volume, of a master cylinder differs depending on the size of the piston (all other factors being equal). Pressure equals force/area. So a piston with a small area will create relatively high pressure, but the trade off is the low volume of fluid displaced. When you get to the other end of the brake line, the caliper is in the opposite end of the same basic relationship. Force equals pressure times area. So you want lots of piston area to create correspondingly high braking force. Now you need more volume however, to move all those pistons. What it comes down to is making sure you have a master cylinder matched to the number of calipers and pistons hangin' on the front forks.

BRAIDED LINE

The nice thing about buying upgraded brakes is the fact that you almost always get both better performance and better looks. Braided brake line is another case in point. When you press on the master cylinder lever and create pressure you want all that pressure applied to the pistons in the caliper(s). The laws of physics tell us you cannot compress a liquid. In theory then, the full pressure created at the master is applied to the pistons – unless the walls of the rubber brake lines swell and steal away some of the pressure. Besides looking cool and being more durable than rubber hoses, the braided lines (with a super tough Teflon inner hose to actually carry the fluid) don't swell at all, which provides more pressure at the caliper and a better feel at the master cylinder.

These hoses come in DOT and non-DOT approved forms. Because we're talking about factory bikes, it's relatively easy to get hoses of the correct length made up with the right ends. A lowered front end however, especially when combined with new bars, will require a new front brake line. The easiest way to resolve the dilemma is to buy a line of the right length with a "universal" fitting on either end that will match up to the correct fitting. You can also have a hose made up to any length, with nearly any combination of fittings, at a good custom bike-building shop.

A Fluid Situation

The fluid running through the brake lines isn't just brake fluid. There are at least three types of brake fluid, including silicone-based fluid which is what Harley-Davidsons have run for years and years. It has the advantage of not peeling the paint off any sheet metal it's spilled on, and being less prone to absorbing water over time. It's not a good idea to mix the silicone fluid with the more common glycol-based brake fluids, which as we said isn't a big issue with any current products from Milwaukee.

Rotor Materials

Brake rotors can and are manufactured from stainless steel, cast iron, even ductile iron. GMA in particular offers rotors manufactured from cast and ductile iron which offer a better coefficient of friction – a surface the pad can more easily grab onto. Cast iron rotors are now available with a flashing of chrome nickel to improve their aesthetics. Most of the rotors you see in the catalogs however, and on the street, are made from stainless steel.

Likewise the pads are made from different materials. What are sometimes called organic pads,

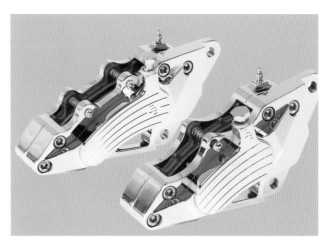

Like many brake manufacturers, JayBrake makes billet calipers in 4 and 6 piston designs. Be sure to use high quality bolts to attach these to the forks. B.C.

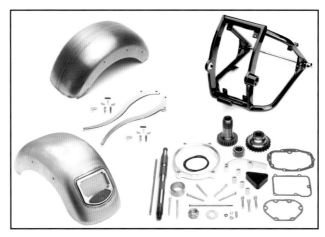

The popular Phatail kit from PM includes a new swingarm, fender and all the hardware needed to convert your Evo or T-C Softail to a 250 rear tire.

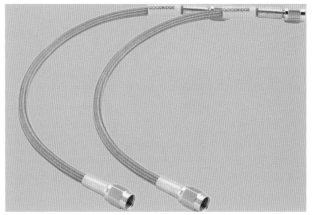

Braided brake lines have both a functional and an aesthetic benefit when used on your Softail. Most can be purchased in nearly any length and matched up with an impressive array of fittings.

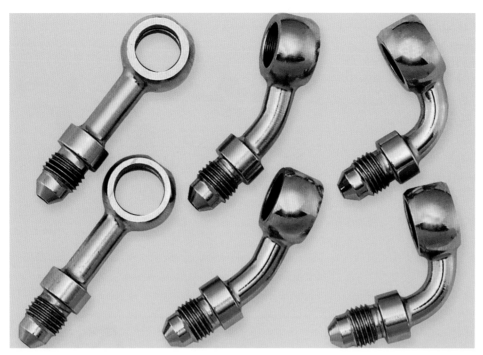

These are only some of the fittings available for universal style braided brake hose. You do have to be sure the fitting is designed for the hose.

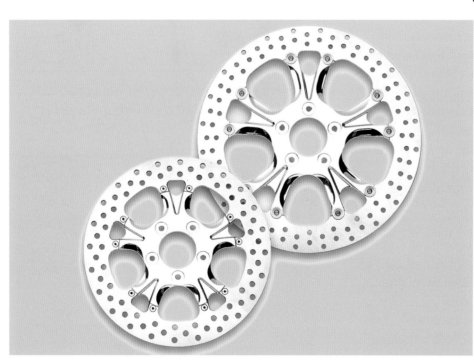

Brake rotors come in a variety of materials, from stainless to cast iron, though the majority by far are made from stainless.

including Kevlar, are softer and better suited to use against the softer cast iron rotors. Sintered iron pads are a good combination for stainless steel rotors. Obviously what you want is good braking without damage to the rotor. Doubts about the best pads can best be answered by a good tech at the company that manufactures the rotor or pad, or the counter person at the shop where you're buying all those polished and plated goodies.

New calipers should be centered over the rotor, this is why they give you those thin, hardened washers. Be sure to use the supplied hardware when bolting rotors to hubs and calipers to lower legs. If you don't, or can't, use bolts supplied with the caliper be sure the mounting bolts are at least a Grade 8, as the full force of a panic stop is transmitted to the frame through the bolts.

Buying brakes is a matter of matching all the parts: the diameter of the master cylinder and the size/number of caliper pistons, pad material with rotor material, your desire for sexy parts with your budget.

TWIN CAM AND EVO

Before discussing the installation of really fat tires on your Softail, it's necessary to digress and mention again the change that took place in Softail chassis with the introduction of the Twin Cam engine starting in model year 2000.

Now, instead of having a separate transmission bolted

to the frame on separate mounting pads behind the engine, the transmission is a nearly integral part of the engine.

The problem that occurs when you try to go past a 150 or 180 tire in a stock frame is the simple fact that the tire runs into the belt (in some cases you can convert to a narrower belt or chain). In order to move the pulley outboard on an Evo bike the transmission can be moved outboard, which means adding an offset mounting plate under the tranny and a spacer between the inner primary and the engine. That strategy doesn't work so hot when you can't move the tranny as a separate part of the drivetrain. Thus the aftermarket wide tire kits meant for 2000 and later Softails include a longer mainshaft in order to move the pulley outboard.

Hands-on mechanics and bike builders report that you can take a stock Softail up to about a 180 tire without major surgery.

In the case of a Twin Cam Softail, one model of the new bikes comes with a 200 tire (and a very narrow belt). Brian at St. Croix H-D reports that the 200 and non-200 tire Softails use the same frame, but a different swingarm, fender, belt, wheel pulley and some hardware. Brian figures you can retro-fit the new parts onto an older T-C frame and run a 200 tire, "but it's still going to be a lot of work."

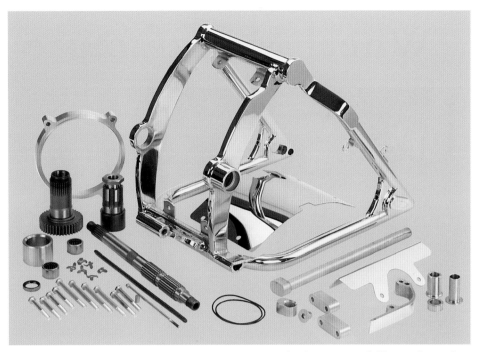

The Twin Cam Softails are very different from the earlier Evo models, especially when it comes to adding a wide tire kit. As shown in the kit above, T-C Softails need a longer mainshaft to move the pulley outboard enough to clear the new, wider tire. Ness

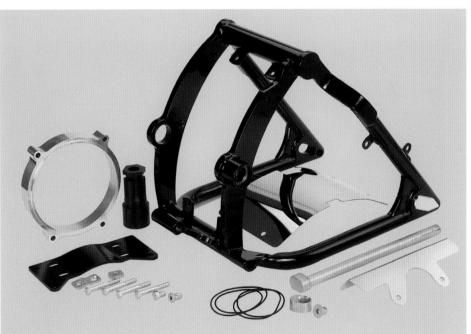

Evo Softails use a separate engine and transmission, so it's possible to move the tranny to the left with a kit like that shown, while leaving the engine in its stock location, and thus get the transmission pulley moved over far enough to clear the fat tire. Ness

Wheel Manufacture at PMFR

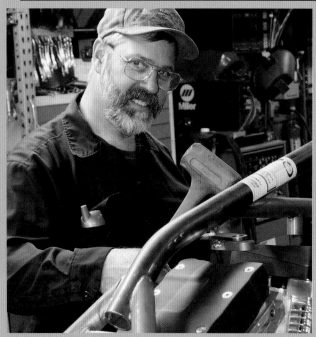

John Trutnau, the man who never uttered the words: I can't, and instead gets involved in a very wide variety of projects from Metric drag race frames to V-twin wheels.

To get a better handle on how motorcycle wheels are manufactured we paid a visit to PMFR, located in Shakopee Minnesota, just west of the Twin Cities. Once in the door you realize that John Trutnau, owner of PMFR, is into a lot more than just wheel manufacture. Walking through the shop to the "wheel department" is a little difficult as you have to detour around various tables and jigs, all of which hold projects in various states of completion. And then there's the four-cylinder drag bike on the floor, no body work yet, just a rolling fame with mock up motor and transmission. The more you look, the more you realize that race-bike components and projects seem to occupy much of the floor and shelf space at PMFR. In fact, many of the top drag race teams are running with frames built at the PMFR facility. In between all the other projects John does complete V-twin powered bike builds, either for himself, or certain special friends.

As John explains in his interview, he was always hangin' out at the drag strip and pretty soon began to make parts for racers, especially parts like wheels that were always in short supply. From ultra light and strong race wheels to street wheels is only a short trip, and today the street wheels are a big part of PMFR's total business. Some people talk a good game, always bragging about all the things they know how to do and just how f-ing cool they are. John Trutnau is the opposite, quietly manufacturing motorcycle frames, wheels and components to very high standards.

On the left is a 10X18 blank as it comes in the door at PMFR. On the right, a finished wheel, designed on the auto cad, cut on the CNC mill, and polished, all operations done in-house.

Wheel Manufacture at PMFR

Q&A: John Trutnau, PMFR

John, give us a little background on you and how you learned to manufacture wheels and all the the other parts you make.

I liked motorcycles when I was a kid and pretty soon I started working on them in my garage at home. When the garage wasn't big enough any more I rented a building, we've moved three times since then. I always went to the national drag racing events and mingled with the racers. When I started to build parts, I developed a philosophy: If you're going to build something, build it better than the competition. We made drag racing components that you couldn't buy any place else. There was a period where you couldn't buy race wheels for example, they were always back ordered. So I started building wheels. Then people with street bikes wanted wheels so I started doing that. Street bikes make up 75% of my business now. In terms of my training, I went to Vo-Tech for welding, but otherwise I'm self taught.

Do all wheel companies start with the same one-piece blank, if not, what are the differences?

A front wheel in the CNC machine, it will probably take an hour to do all the machining operations.

To perform all the machining operations, from rough cuts to finish work necessary in the production of a wheel, requires an impressive array of tooling.

Wheel Manufacture at PMFR

PMFR uses blanks produced by a rotary forge, then mounts them in their own CNC machine for the various machining operations.

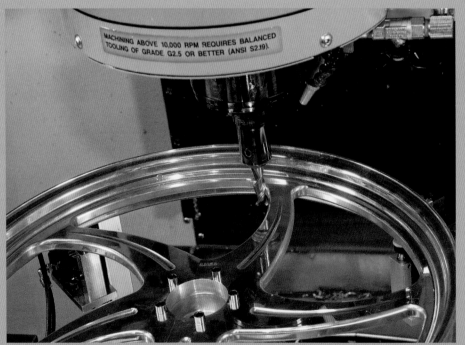

A close up shows the tooling as it works on the inside radius of a spoke. Cutting a wheel from start to finish requires changing tools a number of times.

There is more than one place to get a blank, but everybody is pretty tight lipped about their source. No one will tell you where the blanks come from, though it's starting to open up a little. There are four vendors in the US, the more expensive blanks are better. Centerline is one of the big providers, they have a distributor and you have to go through that distributor.

Apparently there are two ways the blanks are formed?

Yes, there's what they call split and spin. The other method uses a rotary forge. With split and spin they take a raw disc of aluminum, mount it in a fixture where it spins, and then come in with a tool that splits the disc and forms the rim. The other method uses a rotary forge. Both blanks start out as 6061 aluminum, and both are heat treated to a T6 grade after the initial forming is done.

What about cast wheels, are they as good as a billet wheel?

A cast wheel is like a sponge, it's hard to plate due to the porosity. Cast wheels are also harder to machine because they don't have flat level surfaces for the tooling to work on.

Wheel Manufacture at PMFR

are three processes and three washes between. The buffing compound is animal fat, so you have to cook it off with 180 degree water, I had to have my own washing machines made

The only thing we don't do is the chrome plating, we send the wheels out of state for that. It takes special tooling to ensure the chrome gets down into the inside corners.

One of the CNC machines cutting the spokes for a PMFR competition wheel.

Are the one-piece wheels we all run now lighter than the two or three-piece wheels we had on the street a few years ago?

The one-piece wheels are generally cheaper and stronger, but they aren't necessarily lighter.

How does a typical consumer tell the difference between a good wheel and a so-so wheel?

When I buy something I spend time on the Net doing research and asking questions. The consumer needs to fish that information out for himself. Most of them are good wheels, you do get what you pay for.

Other than the blank, do you do all the manufacturing in-house.

Yes, we design the wheels on our auto-cad program, then cut them on our own CNC machines. Even the polishing is done in-house, we had to make all the tooling and the jig that holds the wheel. There's actually more time in the polishing than the machining. For example, there

John had to figure out more than the machining, he also had to build and adapt the polishing equipment seen here. The "handle bars" are a nice touch.

Chapter Four

Project Softail - The Bobber

Powder Coating and Lacing the Wheels

In order to make our Project Softail look more like something from the 1960s we decided to paint the rims black. Though it might seem that we could have simply scuffed the rims to knock down the shine and then spray painted them black, anyone who has tried that trick soon finds that the paint chips easily, leaving the chrome showing through underneath. Powder coating, however, leaves behind a much more durable finish. We took the rims to Kangas

Our finished wheels, after lacing, with the "new" powder coated rims. Note the nice finish on the powder coating.

Enameling, where Curt Kangas started the process by cleaning them thoroughly. Though sand blasting sounds like good preparation, "it can cause the plating to lift," explains Curt.

WHAT IT IS

Power coating is the somewhat new means of coating metal objects with an extremely durable finish sure to withstand the rigors of life on the road. The material is a polyester powder, and the "spray painting" has more in common with the chrome plating process than it does with conventional liquid spray painting.

The gun puts a charge on the paint particles, which float through the air in a soft mist, attracted to the object being coated by the voltage difference between the paint and the object. Once coated, the rim or chassis parts, which are suspended on big racks, are rolled into a huge oven. The heat causes the powder to melt and bond to the metal object.

Excess powder is collected at the back of the booth, which is more like a three-sided shed than a conventional paint booth. Excess powder is collected in the filters and periodically baked into a brick. Disposing of the brick is easy as it's inert and totally non-toxic. All the hassles of fresh air hoods and rubber gloves, necessary for painting with modern urethane paints, are eliminated.

The polyester powder comes in a wide variety of colors, including candy and clears. Candy and/or clear can also be coated on top of a part that's already nickel or brass plated. Though it may not replace liquid paint anytime soon, the process gets better year by year.

A new booth and "paint gun assembly." The powder is kept in the hopper (large chrome barrel) where air is used to keep it "fluid" and move it to, and through, the gun itself.

59

Here you can see how the powder floats slowly to the object being coated.

Next stop, the large oven. Time and temperature are determined by the parts and the powder.

Finished rims just out of the oven.

If powder coating has a downside, it's the somewhat rough surface that it commonly leaves behind. The orange peel is acceptable for industrial parts, but not for custom motorcycle components. Curt, owner of Kansas Enameling, used a special powder for our rims. "I had to special order it," explains Curt. "The material is called Super Wet Black and it lays down really nice and retains that super glossy wet look."

Powder coating motorcycle parts requires extra attention to detail, like knowing which powder to order for our rims, understanding how to get the powder to adhere evenly to all the nooks and crannies of a motorcycle frame, and knowing which parts of the object should be masked off with high temperature "masking tape" that will withstand the rigors of the 400 degree oven.

If you're looking for someone to do powder coating of your motorcycle parts, it's best to ask around. Each area has a shop where they understand the idiosyncrasies of coating motorcycle parts. Usually because, like Curt, they build and ride motorcycles.

Here Curt takes off the masking material he put on the inside of the rims before coating.

Wheel Lacing at Kokesh MC

With black rims, two hubs, and two bundles of spokes we headed for Kokesh MC, located north of Minneapolis, to have them reassembled into usable wheels. Lacing a set of wheels isn't rocket science, but it is one of those old-school arts that's quickly being lost in this age of billet wheels.

"Bug," longtime Kokesh employee, started by laying out all the parts and supporting the rim on two pieces of wood. At his right Bug placed the service manual, a useful guide in setting up the initial relationship between the hub, spokes and rim. "The holes in the rim are heavily dimpled at an angle," explained Bug. "So it would be hard to get these rims assembled one spoke off."

Once the spokes are in place on one side Bug flips the wheel and inserts the spokes on the other side of the hub. If all the spokes are in their correct locations, each will have the same amount of thread showing. If a group of spokes are somehow "longer" than the others, it's time to re-think the set up. These are all new or nearly-new components and they screw together easily. "Stainless spokes often come with a tube of thread lube," explains Bug, "and I'm careful to use the lube they recommend."

"Get them in place, then flip the rim, follow instructions again. The manual is a good guide, if you follow what it says you should be OK. For some of them there isn't much room to swing the spokes and turn the nipples. If it was painted you would likely end up chipping the paint, the powder coat is a better way to go."

The process continues after the wheel is flipped over. In this case the spokes are stock H-D items, but for custom applications, Bug recommends stainless spokes rather than chrome, "because we seem to get less breakage with stainless. And people have to remember to always check the spokes at 1000 and 5000 miles. At least tap each one to be sure they sound the same."

Once the wheel is "assembled" Bug can get it ready to put in the jig for truing.

THE JIG'S UP

Once all the nipples are finger tight the rim is set in the jig as shown. Bug identifies four equally spaced groups of spokes, and will use these to adjust the rim so the side to side motion is minimal and the radial runout is close. Next, he uses an electric screwdriver to snug down all the other spokes. Now he tightens all the spokes evenly going around and around, until they are all tight. "Then I go back and do the final true," explains Bug.

For the final truing Bug makes sure the four groups of spokes have the same amount of threads showing on each one and that the offset is correct. "Each rim has a specified offset," explains Bug. "The manual says the offset for this Standard Softail should be between 1.665 and 1.685 inches. So I measure from the hub to the edge of the rim" (note the photos).

Bug measures and adjusts the offset four times, at each of the marked group of spokes. He loosens two (loosen first) and tightens the other two the same amount, to get the rim to go in the right direction. Once the offset is correct at the four locations all the spokes are tightened to the same tension, "plus one flat."

"Now I take off all but one marker," explains Bug. "I figure everything off the one set, that will be my stop and start point. Getting the radial runout true is harder than the side to side, but it all needs to be done together. For the final truing some people use a pointer, I use a dial indicator. Harley says .030 inch or less for both the side-to-side and radial run out. I get the side–to-side close, then the radial where it should be," explains Bug. "Then I come back and fine tune the side to side run out. This one won't be too tough because the rim is in good shape."

Note the 4 groups of spokes marked with tape, and how Bug does much of the initial tightening with a socked wrench on the base of the nipple.

Offset is measured from the hub to the rim as shown, in the 4 locations.

Next, the dial indicator is installed and set up to measure side-to-side runout.

Once the side-to-side is close Bug switches the orientation of the dial indicator to check the radial runout.

Bug follows H-D specs, which call for less than .030 inches of runout for both side-to-side and radial.

As things get closer, Bug leaves only one group of spokes marked as his stop and start point. At this point the adjusting is done with a spoke wrench.

Truing wheels requires patience because, "you really have to work on both the side-to-side and the radial runout at the same time."

Chapter Five

Chassis Modifications

How Low Can You Go

For most Softail owners, modifying the chassis means lowering the bike. There aren't many vehicles that don't look cooler when they're closer to the ground and the modern Softail is no exception.

Lowering has its cost however. When you take a bike with only three inches of travel and eliminate up to one-half of that travel you're asking for trouble. First, you've taken a chassis that's pretty close to the ground to start with and placed it even closer to the ground, meaning you're more likely to drag

Built by Brian Klock and krew for Mark Missildine, this "newstalgia" Duo Glide sits in the weeds, literally. In this case the lowering is both visual (the front fender is lowered on the fork, the rear is extended) and literal (a one-inch lowering kit in front and Legends air-suspension in back). The bike started as a 2001 Fat Boy.

things through corners and over speed bumps. Second, you are now asking the suspension to absorb the energy of a given bump with considerably less travel. The ride will suffer.

Before jumping into the specifics of shock absorbers and fork springs we need to mention a phenomenon often called virtual lowering. Detroit does it with fender flares and body molding kits that move the sheet metal closer to the ground. Two wheelers can accomplish the same visual lowering with tail dragger fenders, long straight exhaust pipes close to the ground, and even something as simple as horizontal graphics on the tank and fenders. Sissy bars and tall windshields have the opposite effect.

RAKE AND TRAIL

A discussion of Chassis Basics should include a short explanation of rake and trail. Rake is the angle of the front fork, as compared to vertical, while trail is the distance between the front tire's contact patch and the point where the centerline of the bike's steering axis meets the ground (check the nearby illustration). Most factory bikes come with four to six inches of trail, generally closer to four than six. Positive trail, as shown in the illustration, gives the bike its stability and you the ability to ride "no hands." With little or no positive trail the bike can be dangerously unstable. Too much trail gives them a heavy feel in turns, especially at slow speeds, and a tendency to fall into the turn.

The Evo-style Softail chassis shown bolts the engine and transmission to the chassis as separate components separated by an integral vertical frame tube. Twin Cam Softails bolt the transmission directly to the back of the engine case and use a bolt-in vertical member (see page 129).

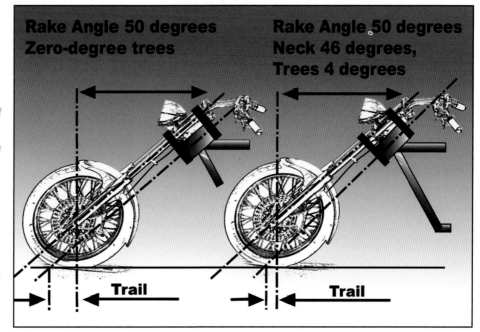

Both bikes have the same fork rake, yet the trail figures are very different. The illustration is intended to illustrate the fact that raked trees are often used in "chopper" situations to reduce the trail to a more reasonable figure. When used on a stock frame a set of raked trees can reduce the trail to a dangerous figure.

With the inertia valve on a Progressive shock closed, the oil is forced to go through smaller orifices and thus give a firmer ride. Biker's Choice.

When the rake of a frame is increased to 38, 40, or more degrees, the trail often goes well past six inches. Experienced builders often use raked triple trees in combination with a raked frame to increase the rake by an additional three or five degrees and decrease the trail back to a more reasonable range. The danger comes when inexperienced owners or builders use raked trees on stock factory frames as a way to increase the rake without having to cut and weld the frame. The net effect of raked trees on a stock frame is to decrease the trail figure to less than four inches, and create an unstable bike. So, don't use raked trees on a stock frame. And if you're having Donnie Smith or an experienced shop rake the frame, ask them for advice as to the need for raked trees. As a reference, the Perse Performance web site (perseperformance.com) contains a trail calculator, and the Drag Specialties catalog contains a chart that serves the same purpose.

A DISCUSSION OF SHOCKS AND SPRINGS

The "shocks" used on most motorcycles combine shocks and springs into one unit but it's easier to understand how each works by looking at the components separately.

If you compress a spring and let it go it bounces back past the original position and through a series of diminishing oscillations before coming back to the starting point. In order to dampen those oscillations a shock absorber (technically these are dampers not shocks) is used.

Looking at a modern shock it's easy to imagine a piston attached to the pushrod, moving through a cylinder filled with oil. The viscosity of the oil, its quality and the size of the hole(s) in the piston are the major factors affecting the stiffness of a particular shock absorber. While the idea of a hydraulic shock seems simple, modern shocks, especially the good ones, are very sophisticated. You want different amounts of damping on compression and rebound. When you hit a big bump the shock should compress very rapidly. If it doesn't you could be tossed off the bike. The rebound valve must react quickly as well, but the goal is to keep the wheel on the ground after you've hit that big bump.

At the risk of getting too deep into the land of engineering, the compression damping controls the

A big bump opens the inertia valve allowing the oil to move faster through larger orifices, resulting in a softer ride. Biker's Choice

unsprung weight - how fast will the wheel and tire move up toward the rest of the bike. The rebound damping controls the weight of the bike (sprung weight) and helps determine how fast the spring pushes the wheel and bike apart after you've hit the bump. Obviously it would be nice if the shock absorber could move quickly when you hit a big bump and more slowly for smaller bumps. The best shock absorbers do in fact have valves that vary the size of the hole that the fluid moves through as the piston travels through the oil. At least one company, Progressive, has taken this concept to the next level with their Inertia Active System that changes the valving depending on the speed with which the suspension components are moving. The best of both worlds, the shocks can absorb the small irregularities as well as the big bumps with minimal tradeoffs.

ANATOMY OF A SPRING

Compared to a shock absorber, a coil spring seems a pretty simple device. Yet, simple or not there's more here than meets the proverbial eye. Coil springs are rated in weight/distance, how many pounds of force does it take to compress the spring one inch? The simplest springs are linear in their strength. If 200 pounds will compress the spring one inch, then 400 pounds will compress the same spring two inches (up to a certain limit). Some springs are progressive, meaning the coils are wound tighter on one end than the other, which essentially creates a spring with a variable rate. On soft bumps you compress only the more tightly wound coils. On harsh bumps those coils bind quickly leaving you with a spring that is essentially much stiffer and better able to handle the larger bump.

LOWER YUR REAR

Most riders don't give a damn about spring rates or damper design, they only want that sucker right down there on the ground. Before buying lowering kits or air shocks, consider the fact that not all Softails are

created equal. The first significant change to the chassis came in 1989 and the next change, more like an overhaul, came in 2000. So there are three versions of the shocks. Be sure to use the right shock on the right frame, especially between the two earlier versions, as damage to the shocks will result otherwise.

When it comes to lowering the back of the bike, there are way too many options. Everything from adjustable air-ride systems to shocks that can be adjusted for height to add-on threaded "lowering kits" that attach to the factory shocks.

Perhaps one of the most popular options is also the least complicated: a pair of high quality shocks from a company like Progressive or Works that allow you to manually set the ride height wherever you want it (within a range). Most of these shocks start out as higher quality shocks than those offered stock and offer better spring and damping rates, so the ride is noticeably better. Many offer a preload adjustment similar to the adjustable spring collar on conventional motorcycle shocks

Among the air suspended systems there are two major choices. The first successful system on the

The Airtail system from Progressive Suspension combines one air-shock adjustable for both ride height and ride quality, and another conventional shock absorber. Kuryakyn

When installed in a conventional fork, the Gold Valve Emulators help the fork emulate the damping behavior of sophisticated cartridge forks. CCI

All the better shock absorber companies make premium shock absorber with built in lowering kits. Biker's Choice

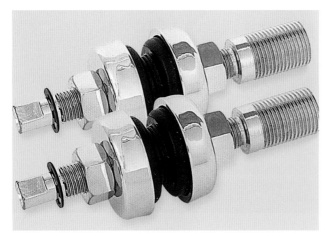

These adjustable lowering kits add onto the stock or aftermarket shocks in your 2000 and up Softail. Biker's Choice.

market came from Legends and is based on two air chambers made by Gates, similar in construction to the big air bags used by heavy duty trucks. The system features an on-board compressor so the ride and ride height can be adjusted on the go. An air release button lets you drop the air for that really slammed look while cruising slow or while parked at the local watering hole. Proponents of air suspension are quick to point out the fact that air makes a near-perfect spring, as it's very progressive. That is, the more you compress it the more it resists further compression.

The other popular air-suspension system is the Airtail from Progressive Suspension. The Airtail uses one conventional shock (like most motorcycle shocks, this is a shock/spring combination) and one "air shock." The air shock is actually a two-chambered device, one chamber controls the quality of the ride and another controls the ride height.

Progressive feels the two-shock approach offers a number of advantages, including the fact that you are actually riding on a conventional spring/shock, which will hold up the bike no matter how much air is, or isn't, in the system. The standard "shock" does in fact include a high quality shock absorber, something that's missing from some other systems. With this design you don't need an on-board compressor (though one can be purchased as part of the kit) if you just want to add air to either chamber with a hand pump or small compressor.

Some professionals like Arlen Ness avoid air suspension because, "if they aren't set up right, when the suspension comes down the fender hits the tire, so what happens if you're riding the bike and you loose the air? I prefer a good shock absorber that lets you adjust the height with a threaded collar." Others, Paul Yaffe in particular, like the air suspension, with only one caveat, "I like Progressive's Airtail, but they're expensive, like 1500 dollars. So sometimes we use a good pair of shocks that are adjustable, like the adjustable shocks from Works Performance

No matter what you buy, be sure it's a brand name product, designed to fit your particular year of Softail. If you buy a high quality shock it's likely to be noticeably better than the stock shocks, which is why some riders replace the shocks - just to get a better ride.

THE OTHER END

We started at the back, now it's time to talk about the front of that motorcycle. First a few terms: Wide-glide and narrow-glide refer to the distance between the two fork tubes. Softails come with a wide-style fork while most Dynas and Sportsters run narrow-glide forks. The fork on your Softail is made up of the triple trees which pinch the fork tubes, and the lower legs, which slide up and down on the tubes. As mentioned earlier, the fork is in fact both a spring and a shock – thus the fork oil contained inside the tube assembly.

For the purposes of this book we're assuming you keep the existing fork, choosing only to lower the front end and possibly add trick lower legs at the same time. The easiest way to lower the front end is with a lowering kit similar to the one we used on our Project Bobber. The catalogs from Drag Specialties, Arlen Ness, Biker's Choice, J&P and all the rest are filled with kits from White Bros. and Progressive Suspension designed to lower the bike up to two inches. The major component in the kits is the main spring, which is shorter and generally stiffer than the stock springs. The better kits come with springs that are progressively wound, as explained earlier in this chapter.

The best shocks use valves that change the size of the orifice the oil is moving through depending on the speed with which the suspension components are moving. Yet, the fixed holes in the typical Harley fork's damper tubes obviously can't change size - unless you install a pair of Gold Valve Emulators from Race Tech. With the installation of these valves the fork will in fact have high quality damping on both compression and rebound. You can even buy the Gold Emulators as part of a lowering kit. We should mention too that the fork tubes used by various Harley-Davidson bikes are not all the same length. In the 41mm family the shortest are the Bagger tubes, followed by the Heritage length and finally the longest found on the Softail Custom bikes.

The caveats mentioned earlier about lowering the rear apply to the front as well. By lowering the front the bike is more likely to drag and less likely to provide a nice supple ride. But then you gotta suffer to be cool, so lower away.

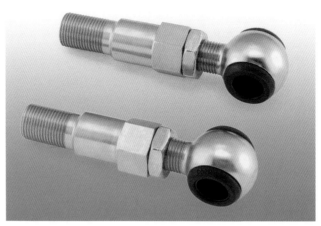

These adjustable lowering kits add onto the shocks in 1989 to 1999 Softails. Biker's Choice

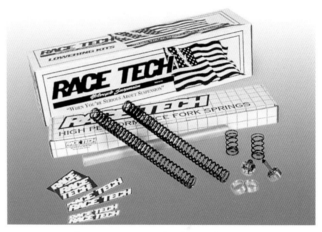

A variety of companies make front fork lowering kits, this particular kit includes a set of Gold Valve Emulators. Biker's Choice

If you're going to disassemble the front end to install a lowering kit, consider the addition of billet lower legs and a flush-mount axle. Biker's Choice

Project Softail - The Bobber

The finished machine, stripped, bobbed and considerably lower than before.

For a variety of reasons, our Project Softail has moved through a couple of shops. For the chassis work, the bike is back at American Thunder. Follow along as we perform a very typical lowering job on what is essentially a typical Softail. The work starts with the bike on the hoist and Ken Misna working to remove the shock absorbers.

Ken loosens the rear mounting bolts before he puts a jack under the Softail's chassis, using a short torque arm on the end of a long half-inch extension. "These are tightened to 120 ft. lbs., explains Ken, "so it can be tough to break them loose."

Once the rear bolts are busted loose, Ken cranks the back of the bike up off the surface of the table and sets a stack of boards under the frame to act as a "safety jack." Now the nuts come off the front of the shocks, the rear bolts are removed and the shocks are dropped out.

Next, the shocks move to the press, where a little pressure unloads the pre-load and allows Ken to remove the snap ring that holds the shocks together. With the outer housing out of the way, it's time to disassemble the shocks per the photos, first busting the top lock nut loose, then (with the help of a little heat) busting the big top collar loose from the shaft.

The rear bolts are loosened with the tool shown, the front nuts are loosened next. Ken puts a stack of boards under the bike just in case the bike slips off the jack while he's wrestling out the shocks. Rear bolts tighten to 120 ft. lbs.

3. *Taking off the extension means first breaking the top lock nut loose from the pre-load collar.*

REASSEMBLE

Ken sets the adjuster part of the new extension (lowering kit) for maximum length, because longer is lower, though he is careful to maintain full thread engagement on the big adjuster nut. The position of the adjustable disc on the shock extension shaft determines pre-load, the adjustment of the big nut on the shaft sets the height.

Ken uses green Loctite on the shock shaft, and screws the pre-assembled extension down onto the shock shaft. Ken used a two-step disassembly process, and likewise this part of the assembly comes in two steps. With the shock extension (or lowering kit) screwed onto the shock shaft, Ken locks the big nut against the collar, and then the collar and upper nut are locked against the shock shaft. The press is used to compress the shock, with the outer housing in place, so the snap ring can be reinstalled.

Installing the shocks into the chassis isn't as simple as it might sound as the additional length makes it more difficult. The first step is to put the bushing

1. *The stock shock, and the two lowering kits.*

2. *Ken compresses the shocks, then removes the snap ring.*

4. *Now you have to heat the collar (to loosen the green Loctite). "I like to clean the threads on the components to remove the Loctite before reassembly."*

5. ...then break the shock extension loose from the shock shaft as shown.

6. The extension can now be screwed off...

8. The press again, this time the snap ring is being installed.

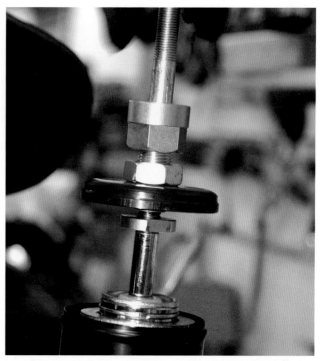

7. ... only to be replaced by a longer adjustable extension, which is locked to the shaft with green Loctite and a two-step tightening sequence.

on the shock shaft and slide the shock into the front mounting holes. Ken had to compress the shocks a little so the big eye at the back of the shocks would clear the cross member and allow him to get the big eyes up into place.

Once Ken finally gets the shocks up into place, it's a matter of placing the rubber cushion on the outer part of the front of the shock, then inserting the bolts in the shock eye at the back of the shock. Ken warns that "you have to put anti-seize on the bolts." It helps to lower the bike a little so the big eye will line up with the mounts on the frame. Tightening the front mounting bolts is easier with the bike jacked up higher so the nuts are more accessible. "You can change the ride height with the shocks in place, "explains Ken, "but it's much easier to set it up when the shocks are on the bench."

As long as the jack was under the bike, it seemed like a good time to install the new wheel with powder-coated rim. The procedure is simple enough (unless you've never done it before) and is best described by the photos. We swapped the rotor and pulley from the old rim on to the new, using red Loctite on all the bolts and tightening them to the factory specifications as noted in the captions.

Once the shocks are installed (a tough thing to photograph) Ken loosens the axle adjusters, takes off the nut and taps the axle out of the bike.

Belt alignment, Ken uses a tool from Revenge Cycle to ensure the axle is the same distance back from the pivot bolts on either side. Belt tension must be set at the same time. Rear axle nut is set to 65 ft. lbs.

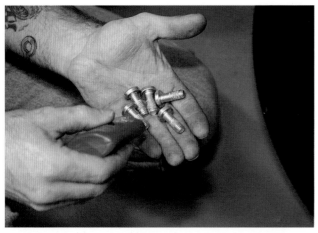

The pulley and rotor off the old wheel are transferred to the new rim. Ken uses red on rotor and pulley bolts. Pulley bolts require 55 to 65 ft. lbs.

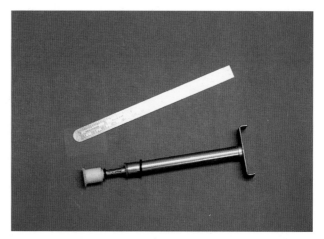

Most mechanics work by feel, but the manual specifies the amount of flex in the belt when 10 pounds of pressure is applied with the tool on the bottom.

Rotor bolts are tightened in a criss-cross fashion to a total of 30 to 40 ft. lbs.

After taking off the caliper, Ken removes the axle and drops out the front wheel.

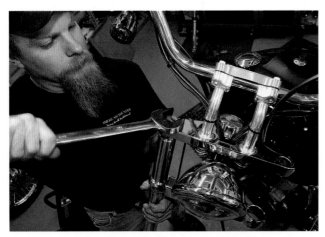

1. After loosening the pinch bolt the upper nut is removed, note the tape on the jaws of the wrench.

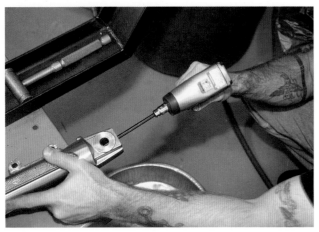

2. The only way to get the bolt out of the bottom of the fork tube is with an impact wrench.

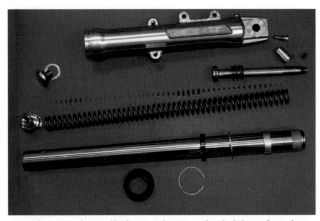

5. This is what all the stock parts look like after disassembly.

Reinstalling the rear wheel takes a certain amount of finesse, as the wheel needs to be rolled into place while the brake caliper is maneuvered around the bulge of the tire and then onto the rotor - and aligned on the swingarm anchor point.

ALIGNMENT PROCEDURE

Ken marks the center of the swingarm pivot bolt and uses a tool from Revenge Cycle to get the axle in the same position on both sides and the belt tension adjusted per the manual, (the manuals differ a little year to year). Ken does the tension check with the bike on the hoist and no rider. Some manuals want you to adjust it to a specified amount of flex in the upper run of belt with a typical rider on the bike. The axle nut is tightened to 65 ft. lbs. and Ken is careful to use a new clip.

FORK LOWERING KIT

Disassembling the fork starts by first pulling off the caliper, followed by the axle and then the wheel. Next, Ken loosens the pinch bolts on the lower triple-trees. Now the top nut comes off, after we put a little electrical tape on the big combination wrench so the wrench won't chew up the nut.

3/4. Once the bottom bolt is out, the boot is removed, followed by the snap ring, then the fork tube is pulled out of the lower leg (on the left). Now the fork tube plug is unscrewed with the impact wrench.

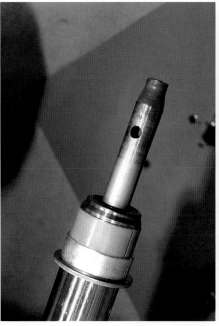

Reassembly starts as Ken drops three top-out springs (for maximum lowering) and then the damper rod down into the fork tube.

Here you can see the damper rod sticking out of the fork tube.

The main spring is dropped into the tube next.

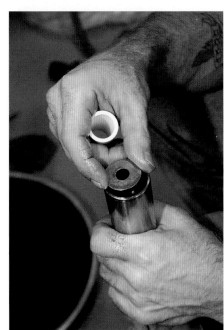

Followed by one of the washers that came with the kit.

The instructions recommend that the plastic sleeve stick out from 0 to 1/2 inch to create the right preload. The sleeve can be cut shorter.

Next in the assembly sequence: one more washer on top of the plastic sleeve (hard to see) and then the fork tube plug.

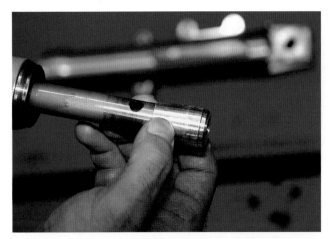

1. Now the lower stop goes on the damper rod...

3. After being coated with teflon sealer, the new bolt and crush washer are inserted and tightened.

4. The slider bushing and spacer are pushed down into the lower leg with the tool shown on the next page.

It's a good idea to put the caps and washers back on the tubes for now so the hydraulic oil doesn't go all over the floor. The bottom bolt, the one that really holds the fork assembly together, comes out with help from an impact wrench. Time now to drain out the fluid and finish the disassembly, which is better described by the nearby photos.

ASSEMBLY

As the service manuals all say: "assembly is in the reverse of disassembly(!)." To make it simpler we've tried to show each step. The lowering kits are not all the same, this kit came with four top out springs and in order to get the maximum amount of lowering we used two top out springs, plus the stock top out spring, in each side. Pre-load of the fork tube assembly is determined by the length of the plastic tube. Our instructions explained that we wanted between 0 and 1/2 inch of tube (plastic) showing past the end of the upper tube.

"You should use a new bolt and crush washer" explains Ken, "and coat them both with liquid

2. ...and the tube is inserted in the lower leg.

5. The tool shown is used to push (first) the slider bushing...

6. ...and then the fork seal (inserted with the letters facing up)...

7. ...into the lower leg as shown.

8. The snap ring and then the boot are the last two steps.

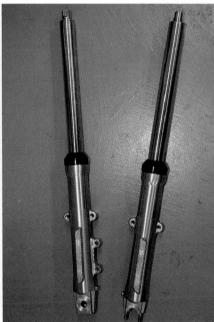

9. The result is two assembled fork tube assemblies.

10. Ken installs 12 ounces of 15 weight fork oil, the same amount and weight as stock.

12. Fork cap nut and sealing washer go on now, nut is tightened before pinch bolt is final-tightened. Sealing washer may need to be replaced.

13. Pinch bolts are tightened to 35 ft. lbs.

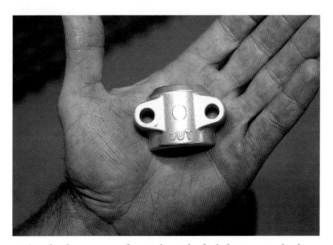

14. The lower cap for right side fork leg is marked but, if it isn't the tapered edge goes to the inside.

11.Ken slips the fork tube assembly up into place.

Teflon sealer. I always clean the screw threads first so the sealer will adhere to the threads."

There are just a few more points to make: The fork seals should always be replaced, they go in with the letter side up and the deeper part of the seal pointed down toward the fluid.

The tubes are filled per the manual, "the lowering kit won't make any difference in the fork's fluid capacity," explains Ken. "If you add new lower legs or chrome lower legs, be sure to wash them out first as they always contain metal filings from the machining and chrome plating operations."

The fork tube assemblies go in next, note the photo sequence. If the sealing washer under the fork cap nut is too beat up it should be replaced.

As was done on the other end, this seemed like a good time to install the new wheel assembly, most of this story is told by the photos.

Final notes: Our bike runs fine without a speedometer. If you want to add a speedo however, the harness to the ignition switch may have to be extended so the other harnesses (speedo and fuel pump) will reach their respective components. Some small bar-mount speedos have idiot lights as well.

Like all motorcycle projects, this one took longer and cost more than we originally planned. Yet, in the end, we succeeded in building a simple customized bike out of a stock Softail, with minimal fabrication and a modest amount of money.

Again, the rotor needs to be swapped to the new wheel assembly, and the rotor bolts (with red Loctite applied) tightened to 16 to 24 ft. lbs.

Ken recommends putting anti seize on the axle. Once the axle is in place the axle nut can be screwed onto the end of the axle.

Loctite isn't needed as the axle nut is a self-locking design. Ken uses a screwdriver to hold the axle so the axle nut can be tightened to 65 ft. lbs.

Then the self-locking nuts for the end cap (which must be installed per the earlier illustration) are tightened to 11 to 15 ft. lbs.

We are finally ready to rock and roll. The beauty of this plan is, mechanically it's still a brand new H-D Softail. We're out of time, but the project could use a small speedo, mini-apes ...

...and blacked out engine components. Ultimately, things like the height of the bars and whether or not to run a speedo or change the pipes is up to you.

Chapter Six

Custom Gallery

Idea Machines

"This is my third attempt at customizing a bike," explains Curt Kangas from Hopkins, Minnesota, with a note of humility in his voice. Yet, if you consider the extent of the work, and the fact that Curt did a large percentage of that work

himself, there's no need for him to be so humble.

The one big job Curt didn't want to do himself is the frame, which went to John Trutnau of PMFR (seen in Chapter Four). Together they stretched the frame three inches and increased the

This do-it-yourself Softail uses a typical hot-rod 80 for power, one with milled heads for more compression, a Crane cam and adjustable pushrods, HI 4 ignition, a re-jetted CV carburetor and a pair of long sweeping straight pipes.

rake to a total of thirty eight degrees. Most builders, especially non-professional builders, would have opted to have the stock tanks stretched to match the frame, or purchased a stretched set of tanks. Curt decided to do the job himself. After teaching himself how to TIG weld he converted the two-piece tank into a stretched one-piece assembly with a raised section in the center. Instead of putting the speedometer on the bars or in a dash, Curt decided to incorporate it into the tank.

First he purchased a piece of steel pipe of about the right diameter, "but it was 5/8th of an inch thick," explains Curt. "So I put it in a lathe and cut it down until it was thin enough to weld to the sheet metal tank, and the right diameter for the speedometer." If all this metal work on the tank sounds difficult, consider that Curt's only metal working tools were a hammer and dolly.

As long as he was getting so good with the TIG welder, Curt decided to do a little work on the Jesse James fenders before installation. The front fender needed only a change in the radius. The rear needed a similar change in radius, more skirting on the sides, and frenched in housings for the taillight and license plate. To lower the fender on the bike, and thus help to lower the whole bike, Curt cut and sectioned the factory fender strut.

The paint is another of Curt's jobs, done with true blue pearl from House of Kolor. Of course, first he had to mold the frame to smooth the welds done

The seat base is Curt's own, created in fiberglass and then sent to a local upholstery shop to be covered in black naugahyde.

John didn't stretch the tank with "tails" at the end, but rather cut the new one piece tank through the middle and added a section. Likewise the top panel, which is part of the tank, not a second skin on top.

in Milwaukee. To create the sweeping handle bars Curt solicited a little help from John at PMFR. Tom Warner from Precision Wheel Service mounted the stock Fat Boy rims in a large lathe and cleaned up the shape, though John Trutnau milled in the "rivets" along the edge.

After looking over this home-grown custom there are only two things to say: Stop being so humble, and we can't wait to see attempt number four.

Deuce With a Difference

When Jerry Crawford asked Donnie Smith to make a mild custom out of his wife's Softail Deuce, Donnie planned all the normal tricks, like a stretched gas tank. "But the funny thing about a Deuce," explains Donnie, "is the gas tank. It's impossible to extend, 'cause the tank is flat on the top and round on the bottom, almost like it's upside down. We played with that and we tried, but you can't make the line work. We finally gave up. Hell, it's a stretched tank anyway,"

The rear fender on a Deuce is just as unique as the tank, so rather than try to fight with the factory design, Donnie and crew cut off the struts and, "added a fender of our own with internal struts, and one of our license brackets on the back." The front fender is a long narrow aftermarket design that wraps tightly around the 21 inch Avon tire mounted to the PM wheel. Bringing up the rear is another PM wheel, this one wrapped by a 180X18 Avon tire. The PM wheels are part of a complete set, meaning the rotors and rear pulley match the wheel design. And of course the four-piston calipers are engraved with that same PM logo.

The bright brandywine paint job is the work of Paint Works, with flames by Lenni at Krazy Kolors. "That's a beautiful paint job," adds Donnie," it really helps to make the bike, I can't stress enough the importance of the paint job." In order to eliminate those unsightly turn signals the crew at Donnie Smith Custom Cycles set small LEDs into the Kuryakyn rear axle covers, and used Kuryakyn mir-

Just because the factory offers the Deuce as their already-customized softail, doesn't mean someone like Donnie Smith can't take it to the next level. Sheet metal changes include both fenders. And as Donnie says, "paint makes the bike."

Gone are the factory fender struts, new fender is supported internally. Donnie squeezed a 180 rear tire in the stock swingarm and kept the belt. Tan seat color compliments the red paint and black frame.

rors with integral lights on the front of the bike.

To power the Twin Cam Jerry took it to Delano Harley-Davidson located west of Minneapolis. The trained technicians there installed a factory 95 inch kit, complete with their #203 cams and ported heads. A Screamin' Eagle filter eliminates any unnecessary restriction on the intake side, while a pair of Reinhart pipes do the same for the exhaust. The end result is a very clean, very tasteful Deuce. One that stands apart from any other while remaining very much a Harley-Davidson.

The No B.S. Softail

When Scotty Riendeau decided to upgrade his Deuce, he knew two things for sure. It had to be fast and it had to be bright. Fast like the other four-wheeled hot rods in his garage. And bright? Well, Scott makes his living selling PPG paint, so there was no point is painting this one flat black.

Shadley Brothers, in Whitman, Massachusetts is the shop Scotty chose to do the work. And work they did. First the bike came down to the bare frame. Next, Mark and crew cut off the the neck and repositioned in with an additional five degrees of rake. To clean up the sheet metal, the boys took the dash and top off the tank, and added a new panel and single filler neck. The other tank, the one that holds oil, received the stretch treatment so it would better fit the frame. Up front a Yaffe fender had to be widened to fit the 21 inch Avon.

The other major part of the project can best be seen from a rear view. What you see is a 250X18 inch tire. The huge rear tire, wheel, swingarm, fender and hardware are all part of the Phatail kit from Performance Machine.

After doing a mock up of the Phatail kit to ensure everything fit, the modified frame, swingarm, fenders and gas tank were all molded to make the welds and seams disappear, then loaded into the paint booth at the Shadley Brothers shop.

The yellow paint, part of the PPG Vibrance line, is a particularly bright hue, known as yella. The orange scallops are the work or John Hartnett, applied with (surprise, surprise) more PPG materials. With the bright part of the equation taken care of, the Shadley

From the fat rear tire to the extra rake up front, this is one Softail that says: "let's race!" There isn't much here that Scotty doesn't need to go down the road.

The more you look the more you see. Like the stretched oil tank, the missing concave hollows in the boomerang, the snug fitting front fender and the first class hardware.

Brothers crew converted the 88 inch Twin Cam to a 95 inch fire breather with high compression pistons, heads from Kendall Johnson and 585 gear-drive cams from Sifton. Air and gas are mixed in the Mikuni carb, fired by direct-mount Shadley coils and exit via the Vance and Hines exhaust.

Mark installed a few nice accents during the final assembly. Things like the Carlinni handle bars, Head Winds light, Chrome covers for the engine and transmission and a custom seat.

Hot Rod Stew from PYO

Paul Yaffe has a recipe for one hot Softail. Start with a stock Softail as delivered from Milwaukee. Cut the neck and set the rake at forty degrees. Now install the factory fork tubes into a set of six-degree triple trees to bring the total rake to forty-six degrees, and the trail back to a more reasonable number. For rolling stock, try a 21 inch Metzeler tire on a CCI rim up front. On the other end install a wide tire kit and 240 Metzeler tire mounted to a CCI rim. Hold it up off the ground with an Airtail suspension from Progressive Suspension. If the whole thing seems to be going too fast, slow it down with RevTech calipers and rotors.

Now stretch the gas tank, add a long sweeping fender up front and a short fat example in the rear. Spray black paint over all the sheet metal, followed by accents in orange and silver. Throw out the stock 88 cubic inch cylinders and pistons, and use 95 inch examples instead. Cap off the cylinders with stock cylinder heads and operate the valves with mild cams. Re-work the Keihin carb and then bolt on a Mo Flo air cleaner and a set of black exhaust pipes. Stick with the tried and true five-speed transmission.

Once the whole thing is out of the oven, garnish with more items from the PYO cook book. Things like the Choppa Bars and Power mirrors, and a Chopper license plate holder and taillight. Don't forget the CCI headlight, a seat from Guy Tieman and gauges from Dakota.

Paul Yaffe got a lot of bang for the buck when he built this tasty Softail. Other than the extra rake, the bike is based on bolt-on parts from the PYO catalog.

Paul has his own ideas about paint colors and often uses some form of H-D colors when customizing factory bikes. In this case the color combinations work with a black frame.

When you're all done, take it down to the local waterin' hole for a test. Most tasters will agree the results are spicy without burning your tongue (or wallet). The nice thing is, with the exception of the frame work, it's a recipe anyone can make with mostly PYO parts. Just add cash and hard work. If your hot rod stew doesn't turn out to look exactly like this one, well that's OK, because a good cook needs to be creative.

You might be looking at Bob Belanger's flamed bike and wondering, "what the hell is a Bagger doing in a Softail book?" What you don't realize unless you take a closer look is that Bob Belanger's bike is actually a Twin Cam Softail disguised as a Bagger. Bob (aka Be Bop) explains that it all started when he bought the year 2000 Softail. "I bought a new Softail standard and right away had Prep Performance in Quebec, do the motor. They punched it out to 95 cubic inches, ported the heads, put in some good cams and a six speed transmission from Baker. Once I had all that work done I gave it to Dave Perewitz, he and I decided to make a Bagger out of the Softail."

Starting at the front, the Cycle Fab crew installed a Road King front end, complete with the factory headlight nacelle. Behind that sits the stretched tank with matching stretched dash. And a little lower, the stretched and paneled oil tank. The rear bags and fender are all part of a kit from Daytec.

Rather than use billet wheels, Bob insisted on straight-laced wheels from Hallcraft, a nineteen in front and an eighteen in back. "We put a 180 tire on the rear wheel," explains Bob. "Most people don't realize you can do that without changing the swingarm or the belt, you just have to change the sprocket so the belt doesn't hit the tire."

For paint, Bob chose cobalt blue on everything except the frame, even the front fork and Perewitz

This is one swoopy Custom, one that looks more like a Bagger than a Softail. Dave Perewitz stretched the gas tank and dash, and added an aftermarket front fender from Russ Wernimont.

The nicely shaped bags and rear fender are part of a kit from Daytec. Spoked wheels help it look more like a bagger, rear wheel supports a 180X18 inch tire.

air cleaner cover. On top of the blue is one of Dave's signature flame jobs and on top of that are the multiple clearcoats "This Softail makes a good driver and a good Bagger," explains Bob. "Those Daytec bags are just as big as Bagger bags, because they're deeper, and because we cut out the normally concave inside panels - meant as clearance for the shock absorber. It's a great bike, partly because people don't realize what it is."

Second Time's the Charmer

Like a lot of custom Harleys, Scott Morgan's Springer didn't just appear one day with a stretched frame, bright red paint and 250 rear tire. What Scott calls stage one took place at the Donnie Smith Custom Cycles shop shortly after Scott picked up the year 2000 Softail from the dealer.

Donnie and crew started by adding a new front section to the frame, one that provided an extra three inches of stretch and seven degrees of rake for a total of forty. A longer frame needs a longer tank, taken care of in this case by metal-man Rob Roehl, who stretched the factory gas tank to match the dimensions of the new frame.

To help get the bike down the road, Don Tima installed a 95 inch kit with ported factory heads and the recommended cams from Head Quarters. Breathing through the CV carburetor the engine pulls strongly from 1000 rpm to redline, with a peak of 98 ft. lbs. at about 4500 rpm. The rest of the stage one program included internal shocks for the Springer's springs, and a laser light where the stock fork shock used to mount. GMA calipers and Ness rotors replaced the stock items, and a 19 inch wheel and tire replaced the stock 21 inch Milwaukee hoop.

The custom Harley market moves nearly as fast as the new factory race bike from Milwaukee, and the wide tire phenomenon is a good case in point. There were no 250 tires when Scott purchased the bike. When he saw the first 250 tire and wheel at a trade show a few years after finishing the Springer,

Like Donnie says in his interview (Chapter Two), the big rear tire really helps a bike make a statement. In this case the rest of the bike isn't bad either. Note things like the fender mounted to the swingarm and the polished/painted engine.

Custom seat is designed to compress as the bike goes over bumps. Speedometer is housed in special Donnie Smith handle bars. Scott wanted the headlight moved from the stock location to that shown.

Scott knew it was time for phase two.

Thus the bike made the trip back to Donnie's shop for a new swingarm, wheel, tire and fender, all part of a kit from PM. At the same time Scott changed the paint job slightly with more Kosmos red paint, and a set of what Scott calls "California flames" done in true blue paint with silver metal flake tips. The end result is a factory Springer that looks and handles better than anything to come out of a dealership.

Cindy Mesmer's 2005 Deluxe is her first Harley and in personalizing the bike she decided to stay with the nostalgic theme. Most of the early-style accessories she purchased, and there are plenty, came from the local Harley-Davidson dealer.

Many of the items Cindy added might be called "brighteners" and include basic chrome goodies like the upper and lower fork sliders, chrome rings for the headlight and passing lamps, as well as the turn signals. Cindy rides alone and would just as soon stay out of the wind, so the seat is a solo model and the windshield is a detachable nostalgic model. It's hard to have a custom bike without changing the grips, switch housings, levers and the floorboards, which of course Cindy did, though the half-moon floor boards weren't on the bike at the time of the photo shoot.

Though most owners would automatically lower the bike, the Deluxe comes with the lowest seat height in the Harley line. Cindy's new-old Softail did receive some additional ponies in the form of a Stage One kit installed at the local dealership. The kit consists of a Screamin' Eagle air cleaner assembly with a nostalgic cover, and a pair of Cycle Shack turn out mufflers. In the end, Cindy's old bike goes down the road like a new one, and puts a huge smile on her face at the same time.

Cindy stayed with the classic theme as she added chrome and accessories to her new Deluxe.

The Deluxe now sports a few extra ponies, thanks to a factory Stage One kit, and some extra shine, thanks to things like the spear on the front fender.

Even the windshield comes from what Harley-Davidson calls its "nostalgia line."

The Test of Time

Doug Palfi from Minneapolis could be called a man with a plan. "I didn't do any sketches before building the bike, but I had pictures of other bikes, and I knew I wanted the new machine to be long, low, and fat and fast." Implementing the plan started shortly after Doug bought a 1997 Fat Boy late in 1999.

For the long part of the equation, Doug took the frame to Donnie Smith's shop and requested an extra seven degrees of rake, which also served to lower the front of the bike. To lower the rear a similar amount Doug installed new adjustable rear shocks. The fenders are part of both the lowering job, and the fattening job. Both are extended to pull the bike closer to the asphalt and widened to fit the larger rear tire, as well as Doug's idea of a perfect profile.

The rest of the fat-ness comes from the use of five gallon tanks, stretched to wrap around the seat and radiused to curve over the motor. Any discussion of fat-ness, needs to include the wide beach bars mounted up front.

The wheels are Monaco models from Performance Machine, the same company that provided the six-piston front and four-piston rear caliper. The front caliper is matched to a large diameter floating rotor while the rear is part of a drive-side brake assembly. Both eighteen inch tires came from Avon, the rear is a 180 while the front is a 130. Installation of the 180 rear tire meant use of a wider swingarm.

Lee Wickstrom gets credit for making it fast, by adding more compression, a pair of his own ported

Front fender started out as a Heritage fender before being widened and stretched with a tail section from a Fat Boy rear fender. The rear fender was widened as well, and stretched two inches to match the profile of the front.

The five gallon Fat Bob gas tanks are radiused on the bottom and stretched to wrap around the custom seat. Graphics are the work of Lenni at Krazy Kolors.

heads, a .577 S-E cam and Super G carb. Combined with a Pro Pipe from Vance & Hines, the combination achieved a best of 94 horsepower on the dyno. Pretty good for a eighty-inch Evo.

Finishing his plan took one year, five years later Doug is still getting compliments wherever he stops. Which goes to show you don't have to follow the latest fads to have a good motorcycle. You do need a good plan though, to ensure that the bike looks good the day it's built – and well into the future.

"Woody" owns a car lot in Whiteland, Indiana, so it's only natural that he would have a better-than average motorcycle, in this case a worked over Softail that started life in 1995 as a Heritage model. Though the bike retains all the signature items that go along with a Heritage, like the sixteen inch wheels and classic sheet metal, it also benefits from some updates that help to enhance the bike's appeal.

Woody started out by lowering the bike nearly four inches in the front and back with standard lowering kits. Next came the 80 spoke wheels in place of the standard 40 spoke hoops from Milwaukee.

A light bar borrowed from a Road Glide replaces the standard rear light bar (and drops into the existing fender holes), combined with an aftermarket lens and laydown license plate bracket. The standard fender rails are decorated with a pair of slick marker lights from Kuryakyn. Up front the turn signals, a pair of small bullet lights, are located just under the controls. The controls themselves are mounted on the ends of the mini-ape handle bars. To clean up the stock frame Woody used chrome caps at the ends of the swingarm and more chrome covers in the concave parts of the boomerang.

The Heritage is powered by what we used to call a "hot rod 80" engine, one with more compression, and a cam with more lift and duration. Braided lines replace the black oil lines, and a chrome starter assembly hides under the oil tank.

A good design doesn't need an overhaul, just a little enhancement. The small improvements seen on Woody's bike came from both H-D and the aftermarket.

Many of the items, like the heel and toe shifter and the swingarm covers are from the Kuryakyn catalog.

The motor is a massaged 80 inch Evo, with roughly 80 horses, plenty to pull Woody around Whiteland, Indiana.

Rock 'n Roll Softail

Anyone with a hankering to make a radical ride out of a stock Fat Boy might look no farther than this "Softail" built by Dave Perewitz and owned by Brad Whitford from the Aerosmith band. "The bike started as a Anniversary model Fat Boy that Harley-Davidson presented to the band in exchange for a concert," explains Dave Perewitz. "We stretched the frame a lot, six inches, and set the neck at 38 degrees. Then we used three degree trees and a complete front end from Perse, so the total rake is 41 degrees. At the back of the bike we installed a 250 tire/ Phatail kit from Performance Machine."

The wheels, brakes and controls come from the same company that made the wide tire kit. The slick strutless rear fender came from Performance Machine as part of their kit, though the way it wraps around the custom seat is the work of metal-man Big Ron. While he was at it, Ron stretched the stock oil tank so it better matches the curve of the frame. The gas tank and front fender are both from Russ Wernimont, molded and prepped for paint by the Cycle Fab crew.

"Brad wanted the bike to be a bright green but he didn't want a stock color," explains Dave, "so we started with Prismatique green from PPG and then topcoated that with candy green to get just exactly the right color." For power Dave sent the stock 88 inch Twin Cam to JIMS, where it grew to 117 cubic inches, contained in fully polished cases,

Though a few of the wide-tire kits come with right side drive, the PM kit retains the left side drive. Dave used a PM drive-side brake assembly, and a single front brake mounted on the left side, to leave both wheels open to view from the right.

Just a little bit of curve in the bottom of the Wernimont tank does a great deal to give it more shape and appeal. Handle bar controls are from PM. Twin Cam engine received the full chrome and polish treatment at JIMS.

cylinders and heads. Equally bright is the case for the factory five-speed transmission. The bright engine exhales into a set of simple, curved pipes from TCX.

So if what you have sitting in the garage is a stock Softail, and what you see in your head is a long lean custom, Brad's bike serves as proof that your dream can come true. Though it ain't easy and it ain't necessarily cheap.

Wheels & Tires

Our group of experts, interviewed in Chapter Two, talk again and again about the importance of paint and the impact that new wheels can have on a custom bike. Sheila Hoffman seems to have taken their advice to heart in customizing her Softail Deuce.

The paint is diamond ice, a pearl white color used on late model Cadillacs and applied by Neville Auto Body. To help the paint jump, Sheila asked Steve Wizard to do some nice tasteful graphics, and that's exactly what he did. To protect Steve's work Neville Auto Body finished the job with a series of clearcoats and sanding between those coats to leave Sheila with a perfectly smooth paint surface.

The other major change to Sheila's Deuce is in the wheels. RC Components supplied the Warlock billet wheels, in stock 21 and 16 inch sizes, with a matching belt pulley and brake rotors. To clean it up a bit more, Sheila had Jeff at Namz's Custom Cycle Products install a set of their braided handlebar wiring harnesses, and add a few additional Harley-Davidson accessories.

Sheila's bike works in part because she started out with the most custom of the factory Softails. Also because she spent most of her money in two major purchases, purchases that really help to set her bike apart from all the others – and that's the whole idea.

Sheila only made two changes to her Deuce, but they're both major and both good choices. The paint is essentially white pearl with black graphics, and works fine with the black frame color.

Though the wheel sizes are stock at 19 and 16, the wheels themselves are billet pieces from RC Components with matching rotors and a matching pulley.

The multi-layered graphics are from Steve Wizard, while the braided handlebar harnesses are from Namz Custom Cycle Products.

Chapter Seven

Accents & Accessories

Choose with Care

When it comes to accessories, we are of the less-is-more school. However, they certainly have their place. Things like the small nut covers from Cycle Visions, the swingarm apex covers from Kuryakyn, flush mount axles from Dakota Digital or simply a great set of grips, mirrors and pegs all designed to work together and with the existing design. In fact, that's the whole idea. Pick accessories that compliment the bike without taking over, or taking away from your overall design.

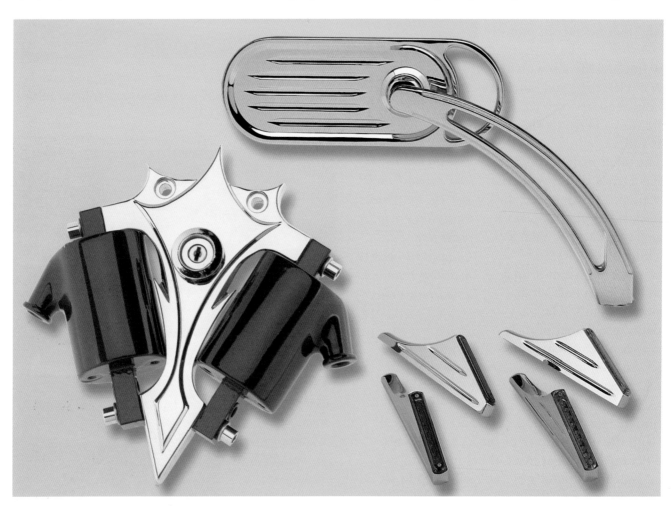

The number and variety of high quality accessories is mind boggling. Whether it's coil mounts from Cyril Huze, an incredible array of mirrors from Arlen Ness or sexy marker lights from Drag Specialties, if you don't find what you need to enhance your ride, you just aren't looking hard enough.

The good thing about the current popularity of Harley-Davidsons and Softails in particular is the abundance of parts currently available from all the major catalog companies, as well as Milwaukee. As we've mentioned before, among the numerous things they're doing right in Milwaukee of late is the accessory and custom parts program. From lights and covers to their own line of pegs and mirrors, the big book from Harley-Davidson contains a huge selection of high quality parts.

LIGHTS, ACTION

Unlike most of the aftermarket, Harley-Davidson offers only lights that are DOT approved. The also offer a wide range of trim ring kits for all the lights on all the bikes. Give the headlight on your Heritage a Frenched look with the extended trim ring, and match the effect on the passing and turn signal lamps with matching rings.

Most of the lights from the aftermarket are not DOT approved, and for most of us it doesn't matter. It becomes an issue only if you live in a state with inspections. What does matter is the apparent legality of the light and related safety issues. Before bolting on the smallest tail or turn signal light ever invented, remember that it might get a negative reaction from the local gendarmes, whether it's truly legal or not. And that a small light is generally harder to see, which is not what you want when the Buick

Everybody wants to get the big ugly factory lights off the bike while retaining some vestige of turn signals. These fender rail lights from Kuryakyn are a great way to do exactly that.

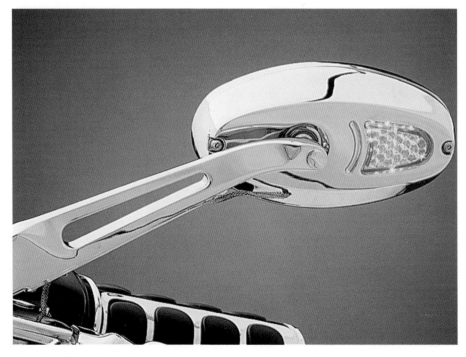

Another Kuryakyn design, these mirrors with integral lights work great as front blinker lights.

Lighting the way, these classy silver bullets are available in two sizes, halogen or LED, and can be used for marker or turn signal lights. Kuryakyn

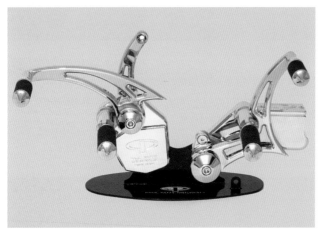

Pick your forward controls to fit your seating position, and match the rest of the controls on the bike. These are part of the Paul Yaffe Collection.

Take a timeless design, the tombstone taillight, and give it a modern twist, complete with light bar for turn signals. Kuryakyn

is coming up quick behind you on a dark and stormy night. LED and halogen lights have the advantage of being bright, even when cased in a fairly small housing. LEDs are nice because they last forever and don't create nearly as much heat as halogens bulbs do.

Side-mount license plates are in wide use and seem to be generally accepted in most states, though you might want to check before bolting one on. Customizer Donnie Smith likes to mount them on the left, as that way they're easier for anyone behind to see, especially if you're in the right lane and the cars or bikes are coming up behind you in the left lane. We can't leave the subject of lights without mentioning the huge variety of bright and beautiful lights from companies like Kuryakyn, Arlen Ness, Drag Specialties and all the rest. There are a thousand ways to replace the big bulky lights on your stock Softail with something smaller and sexier.

Clean it up, especially the all-important front end, with a flush-mount axle from Dakota Billet, available for all the Softail front ends.

LOAD EQUALIZERS

The stock flasher is designed to work with a certain load, or amperage draw. When you eliminate lights from the circuit or replace them with smaller and more efficient lights, there may not be enough load to make the flasher flash. On older Softails the problem can often be corrected with a heavy duty or solid state flasher, one that will flash at a steady state regardless of the load. Harleys with self-canceling turn signals require a load equalizer module however, so the little brain box isn't confused by the too-low current draw.

WIRING

The most important single thing to keep in mind when doing any wiring work can be summed up in one word: neat. Keep it neat, keep wires bundled and grouped into harnesses so they can't be pinched between the fender and frame or melted against something hot or worn through by the tire. In the past we advised our readers to solder the wires as a way to create a durable connection. The down-side to soldering is the way it makes the wire brittle right next to the actual joint. Brittle enough to break later. So if the wires in question are near the engine or subject to vibration, use a crimped butt connector instead. Whether you solder or not, use a piece of shrink wrap on the connection as the final step.

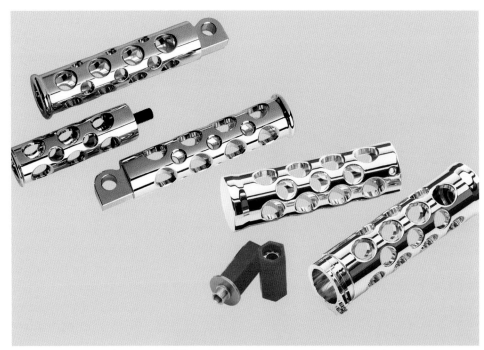

These Battistini-designed pegs and grips bring to mind the efforts of early Bonneville racers to lighten everything in an effort to go faster and faster. Available from Arlen Ness, the grips come with an end-bearing for the throttle, the reduced friction means you can at least open the throttle faster.

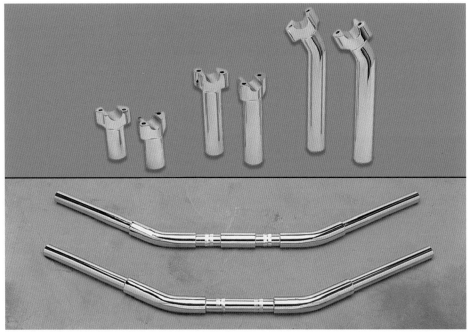

A book could probably be written about bars and risers, they are simply so important to the looks and function of a motorcycle. By using separate bars and risers you have more chance to make subtle changes to the bar position so important to your comfort. Drag Specialties

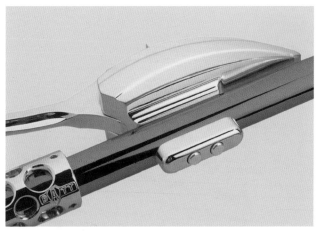

Part of Arlen's Rad II line, these clutch and brake controls include the master cylinder for clutch and brake, and the switches. Note the invisible mounting.

You can't have a custom bike without a custom seat. Pick yours like you would the bars or controls, to fit your fanny and match the rest of the design. Corbin

The grips are as important as any other component on the handle bars. Cyril Huze

THE SEAT

If you're trying to change the profile or slim down the bike, there's no better way to do it than with a different seat. Make the bike a roadster with a solo seat, or at least make it lower and lighter with a slim seat from Corbin or Arlen or one of the many catalogs. We always warn against using a too-long screw or stud to hold down the back of the seat, as it might hit the top of the tire on a bump. Many current builders eliminate the problem altogether by attaching the back of the seat with suction cups or two pieces of hook-and-loop material, though this may leave you with a hole in the top of the factory fender.

If you do use a bolt for the rear of the seat, use a knurled knob or one of the small assemblies with a spring loaded pin (DS-902113 from the Drag Specialties catalog for example). That way when the battery goes dead you won't be looking for someone to borrow an Allen wrench from so you can get the seat off.

Sometimes a single item can define a certain type of motorcycle - a chopper for example. Remember, most cops don't like your hands higher than your shoulders.

Pegs, Controls and Bars

One of the most common bits of customizing most riders do is to change the pegs, controls and/or bars. Black controls and switches can be swapped for chrome with kits available in all the catalogs (some wiring required). Most of these come with extra long leads for those tall handle bar applications. The hot deal is to run the wires inside the bars. Which requires that the bars have a hole where they meet the risers, or that the joint where the bars meet the integral risers be drilled. This also requires that you fish through a wire (on both sides). to pull the harnesses through. Installing new switches and possibly running the wires inside the bars is not a one-afternoon deal. If you're not Mr. Handy when it comes to wiring you might want to get some help for this little project.

Which is not to say you shouldn't change the bars. It's a great way to lower the profile of your ride with flat drag bars or turn it into a chopper with a set of apes. Taller bars require longer wiring for the controls, and a longer hydraulic line(s) for the front brake (and possibly the clutch). Don't forget the throttle and clutch cables. If you're doing all this work take the time to order and install cables that are more than just longer. Cables and lines with braided housings are available in nearly any length from any decent motorcycle shop. Just

Once again providing a new twist on parts we didn't think could be redesigned, Paul Yaffe gives us his skirt blower exhaust pipes with ventilated heat shields. Can be ordered chrome on chrome, or black pipes with chrome shields.

You can really clean up the front of your Softail with a set of bars like these from Paul Yaffe Originals, and still retain mostly of the stock controls.

97

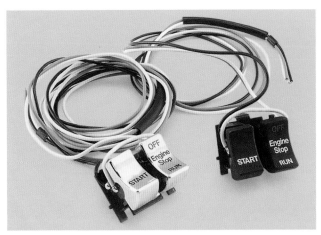

If you're cleaning up the bars, think about the controls and switches. Switches come black or chrome with extra long leads for taller/wider bars. B-Choice

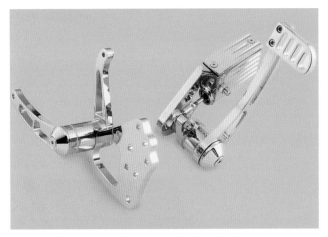

Forward controls often include the brake master cylinder. Be sure the cylinder diameter matches what you took off (unless you changed the rear caliper).

If you want to add some bling to the back of that Softail, consider the multitude of chrome covers from Kuryakyn.

to keep things interesting the aftermarket introduced phat bars a few years back. So now you have to make sure the bars match the risers and any additional accessories that bolt to the bars.

A whole chapter could be dedicated to the various styles of pegs and forward controls that are available. From black with a European style to chrome plated billet, it you don't find something that appeals, you must be blind. It's again a matter of style and taste. Whether you're shopping with Arlen Ness, Cyril Huze, J&P or Paul Yaffe, the catalogs all have matching grips, hand and forward controls. You can really class up your two-wheeled act with some well chosen and matching controls and pegs. If you shop at the big and tall store, consider the fact that some forward controls put your feet farther forward than others. Extensions can also be used to move the controls farther forward. If you like the idea of being able to move your feet around, try a set of floor boards, or install longer boards from Arlen Ness. No matter what you buy remember that the parts have to fit

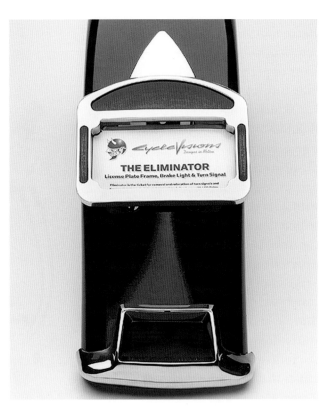

The Eliminator light assembly gets rid of the stock light bar while retaining a turn signal function. The little chrome triangle covers the stock bolt holes.

your plan, and they have to fit you. An uncomfortable bike isn't fun to ride, no matter how cool it might be.

TOURING

Some of us like to have our cake and eat it too. That is, load the bike down with gear for a week-long trip, then strip the rack and windshield off when we get there. Though a number of firms make windshields that can be easily removed from the bike, Harley-Davidson makes some great accessories known as Detachables. Though not cheap, these racks, backrests and windshields are of very high quality and snap on and off with remarkable ease.

And if you want a Bagger built on a Softail chassis, both the Trike Shop and Hoppe offer a "batwing" style fairing that looks much like something off a late model FLH. Built from fiberglass, the brackets (designed for FLSTs) make for easy take off and reinstallation. Combined with a set of aftermarket bags or Harley-Davidson Bagger bags mounted with brackets from Cycle-Visions, you can truly have a Bagger built on a Softail chassis.

When it comes to accessories, the catalogs and web sites offer almost too many options. Remember the wise words of our interview subjects in Chapter Two – who advise you to think before you buy and make sure the things you do buy fit your overall scheme for the bike.

Happy Smith, bother and former partner of Donnie Smith, is a man who likes to ride and ride and ride. Yet, the Softail fits his sense of style and balance better than a Bagger. So Happy did the logical thing, he started with a 2004 Twin Cam Standard, and added a 16 inch factory wheel to drop the front end and put more rubber on the road. Next came the...

...fairing from Hoppe, the bags and crash-bar covers from Iron Bags ("lowers" come off in warm weather) and small luggage rack on the extended Heritage rear fender. All metal work is by Rob at Donnie's shop, with flames by Lenny at Krazy Kolors. If custom means personalized, this is one very Custom Softail.

Chapter Eight

Engines

Hard to have too much

Horsepower is a little bit like sex: a little too much is almost enough and once you've had a bunch it's hard to go back to not having enough. The bulk of this chapter is made up of a 95 inch conversion, because it's the most cost effective way to get a Twin Cam up into the 90 to 100 horsepower range. You need to understand that even the 95-inch sequence presented here, a budget assembly that retains the stock heads and no fancy exhaust, is cheap only in a relative sense.

The V-twin engine is not only the powerplant, it's also the focal point for your motorcycle. If a motorcycle has a soul, this is where it resides. Whether it's the power or the visuals you're after, don't skimp and don't settle for second best.

Obtaining additional horsepower is subject to the law of diminishing returns. It's easy to get the first 5 to 10 extra horses, and not too tough to grab 20 to 30, but after that it gets much more difficult – read expensive.

If budget or taste leads you to a modest horsepower increase, we present various ways to score an additional 5 to 10 horses in only a few hours time. This is what Milwaukee calls Stage One and S&S calls Quick Set Up. We've kept most of these comments to the Twin Cam engines, for at least three reasons. 1. Most of the basic tricks work on an Evo as well as a Twin Cam. 2. Evos are older and likely to have been modified already. 3. The motorcycle press has covered "how to hop up an Evo" pretty much to death.

QUICK HORSEPOWER
S&S Cycle

From S&S Cycle, makers of everything from the classic teardrop air cleaner to the monster 145 cubic inch V-twin, comes the Quick Set Up. By combining the already mentioned air cleaner with a set of their own high performance mufflers, and necessary modifications to either the carburetor or fuel injection mapping, S&S obtains an additional ten rear-wheel horsepower (slightly more with some of the bikes).

For carbureted bikes the kit includes two slow jets, two main jets and a new needle. In the case of EFI

S&S Quick Set Ups promise 10 additional ponies for about $500.00, a deal that's hard to beat. Kit includes classic, free-breathing S&S air cleaner, slip on mufflers and jet kit. S&S recommends that EFI bikes be tuned at the dealer or a certified S&S test facility.

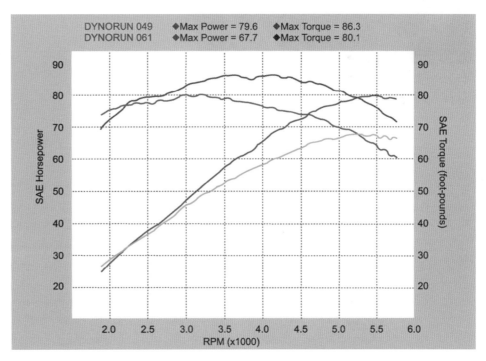

Dyno chart is the result of a Quick Set Up installed on a 2001 EFI Fat Boy, run on the S&S Dynojet dynamometer at the S&S R&D facility.

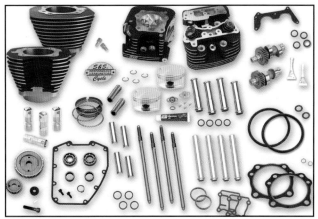

S&S Supersotck 95 inch kit includes pistons, cylinders, heads, and 585 gear-drive cams and adjustable push rods. Expect 100 horses with carb or EFI adjustments.

The S&S VFI tuned runner induction kit is intended to not only eliminate any restriction in the intake system, but provide a mild supercharging effect.

Harley-Davidson offers this Screamin' Eagle air filter kit designed to get as much air into the intake manifold as possible.

bikes, they recommend "that the bike be calibrated by your local dealer to insure that the engine is receiving sufficient fuel." At a retail price of $500.00 (no labor) the Quick Set Up is a very good value in a horsepower per dollar sense.

HARLEY-DAVIDSON STAGE ONE KITS Q&A: DAVE THORSEN, ST. CROIX HARLEY-DAVIDSON

There's an old saying: If you really want to know how something works, ask the person who works with it all day long. We asked Dave Thorsen, one of the factory-trained mechanics working at St. Croix Harley-Davidson in New Richmond, Wisconsin, about the H-D Stage One kits. Dave installs Stage One and Two kits, and does the follow up dyno tests and adjustments, all day long. In fact, we had to reschedule the interview with Dave because on the particular day we planned to drive over to New Richmond, he had six bikes to run on the dyno.

Dave, to start, tell us exactly what goes into a Harley-Davidson Stage One Hop Up?

For Stage 1, the bike stays at 1450cc, but we put on a new high flow air box, slip-on mufflers, and if it has a carburetor there's a new needle and possibly a slow jet change. That's it. The early Twin Cams used a number 42 slow jet like the Evos. The later ones came with a number 45. We just check it and add the 45 jet if it needs it. We always add the richer needle. Even with the needle and bigger jet it can still be hard to get rid of that little spit-back some of the bikes have right off idle. It would be nice if we could change the air bleeds in the carb, that would really help but of course we can't.

If it's a fuel injected bike there's a down load involved. Or we have to install a Race Fueler, or do the whole Race Tuner process (more later). For 2006 all of the Stage 1 bikes will get the Race Tuner.

Is there another step in the hop up process without going to a full Stage 2 kit?

The next move is Stage 1 big bore. We leave the stock cams and heads and just add displacement. These bikes make good cylinder pressure at low rpm and have lots of torque. It's a good package for Baggers. With the lighter bikes we like to give them a cam change too. A download isn't good enough though, you have to do the Race Tuner at this point.

How much additional power do you get with the Stage 1 kits?

With a Stage 1 carbureted bike we get six horsepower at most, usually the bike goes from 65 to 70, or 71 horsepower. The torque goes from 76 or 77 to 80, or 81. If we do Race Tuning of an EFI bike we get a little more than six horsepower.

Give us a quick run down on the Race Tuner and Fueler?

The Race Tuner is essentially software that lets us re-map the bike's fuel and ignition curves. The tuner costs four hundred and fifty dollars plus two hours on the dyno at sixty five dollars per hour. Remember though, on the dyno we are tuning the bike and allowing it to run at optimum levels at all rpms, you are gaining more than just horsepower and torque.

The Race Fueler is two hundred dollars less and doesn't require dyno time, but you can't control the ignition, it only lets you add fuel. The trouble is you have to make the adjustments on the road. The Race Fueler has five fuel adjustments: Three that affect the mixture at high, medium and low rpm, and also an "accelerator pump" control. There is one

A Stage One kit from H-D includes the SE air cleaner kit and a pair of low restriction SE mufflers.

The scanalyzer on top can be used to download a new EFI map from H-D and then install it in the bike's control module. The Race Fueler on the bottom allows the operator to add fuel at various points in the rpm range.

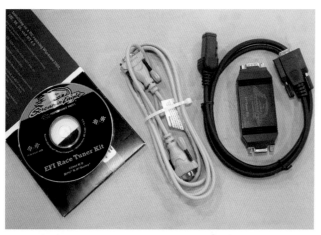

The Race Tuner is H-D's means of remapping both the ignition and fuel curves on late-model EFI bikes.

Wimmer Custom Cycle takes the idea of low restriction breathing and good aesthetics to a new level. The Ultra combines a velocity stack with a cotton filter.

Another Wimmer product, the Spike is manufactured from billet aluminum and comes with an indexable elbow.

more adjustment that affects where the rpm change takes place between high, medium and low. If you're patient and have thoroughly read the instructions you can do a good job with the Race Fueler.

There are also Stage One maps from Harley-Davidson that can be downloaded but they only work in that specific application. You can't deviate from their plan.

Advice from Wimmer Custom Cycle

Lee Wimmer, the man who designs some of the zoomiest air cleaners on the planet, is also a wealth of knowledge and common sense when it comes to doing "Quick Set Up" type hop ups. To quote Lee: "One of the easiest ways to boost performance is to increase airflow and fuel to your motor and then of course be able to remove the spent gases afterwards. Stock motors from the factory have very restrictive air cleaners and exhaust systems. The replacement of the air intakes, and adjustments to the carburetor or fuel injection system, will allow for greater performance for a minimal expense. Wimmer Custom Cycle has been a leader for many years in the intake component department. We have not only designed a great variety of intakes, but have done extensive work on performance as well. There are many options as to style and performance.

"Stage 1 is the first step, and probably the most "bang for the buck" to getting better performance. More fuel in and more gases out will equal more horsepower. There are a few things to keep in mind however. You simply cannot change just one thing without changing another, you need to maintain an air to fuel ratio. Too lean or too rich will lead to problems. Just a quick rule of thumb is to check the color of your spark plugs after running. They should be a gray color. If they are too white you are too lean and this can cause serious problems. If they are black it is way too rich and you will have fouling problems, although this will generally not do damage to the motor. It is far better to be too rich than too lean.

"With carbureted motors you will need to re-jet once you have changed the air box or intake. With fuel injection you will need re-mapping of the ECM. In both cases it is something that should be done by qualified technicians. Re-mapping is definitely something that needs to be done by computer with proper software. Fuel injection systems are becoming much more popular and, in this author's opinion, the direction that the industry is headed. The one thing to keep in mind is when changing the intake you will be adding more air so you need to add more fuel as well. We have gone to great length to do air flow testing as well as actual riding performance for all out products.

A Few Final Words on EFI Systems

A full series of dyno runs, plus the cost of either a factory Race Tuner or Power Commander (or similar product) will set you back an easy five hundred dollars, probably more. There are also a whole raft of products that modify, or allow you to modify, the amount of fuel being fed to the engine at various rpm ranges. A couple of questions immediately come to mind: At what point do I need to do a full dyno run and remapping session? And, is it worth the money?

There are no hard and fast rules. Given the complexity of modern fuel injected bikes, and the amount of money most of us have invested, it seems somehow penny wise and pound foolish to try to skimp on the full dyno run. To quote dyno technician Doug Lofgren from World Class Tuning, "When you change even the air filter the air fuel ratio skews up and down and once you put a pipe on, for sure you need a Race Tuner or full Power Commander session. I recently did training at Fargo Harley-Davidson. Their policy is, if they do even a Stage 1 kit the bike gets a Race Tuner and dyno session. And customers are happy. There are a couple of things to consider here. For one, the stock maps aren't always correct. Partly because the bikes aren't all the same. I've checked a lot of bikes of the same make and I find the fuel delivery is plus or minus five percent, because the fuel pressure isn't always the same. I think it's the pressure regulator, they're inexpensive and the calibration changes over time. Ultimately, most of the people who spend the money on the full dyno session are pleased as punch (assuming it's properly done).

S&S offers two VFI modules, one for Magneti Marelli, one for Delphi bikes ('01 and later S-T all use Delphi). Modules replace the factory unit and offer a number of advantages over stock. Must be installed at an approved S&S VFI Tuning Center.

Exhaust systems, like this set of long straight pipes from Samson, are both part of the bike's style and a big part of the performance equation. D. Specialties

By using the software shown, and the Twin Tec ignition (as used on our first project bike), the operator can design a sophisticated 3-D ignition map.

Chapter Eight Sequence

95 Inch Budget Build

90+ Horses with Stock Heads & Mild Cams

The title of the book is Hop Up & Customize, and the easiest way to get significantly more power from a Twin Cam engine is to install a 95 inch kit. In this case we decided to try a relatively mild kit from Kuryakyn. The kit is based on the idea that by

using carefully chosen parts a 95 inch Twin Cam with stock heads and mild cams can produce very nearly as much power and torque as the same engine with ported heads and much more radical camshafts. The difference between the two engines,

The Kuryakyn budget kit (we supplied the cylinders) is based on additional compression created by the pistons and their 2G gear drive cams. These cams produce substantial power without the need to port the heads. They also use a stock base circle, and thus we could have used the stock pushrods and saved even more money.

besides some measure of power, is money. The Kuryakyn kit does not require ported heads. And because the cams are mild, and based on a stock baseline circle, the stock valve springs are more than adequate, even the stock pushrods can be reused (through an oversight, we did use adjustable pushrods).

DISASSEMBLY

Ken Misna, the bike builder on this project, starts by draining the tank and removing the cross-over tube. Two bolts hold the gas tank on, one at the back and one through-bolt at the front. Don't forget the two-wire connector for the fuel gauge on the bottom of the tank.

Ken removes the exhaust next, the flange nuts are first, then the nuts on the support bracket at the back of the frame on the right side. The air cleaner is removed next, then it's time to move to the left side. First there's the choke cable to take off the bracket, done by loosening the nut from behind, followed by the throttle cables. Before disconnecting the throttle cables, though, Ken puts slack in the cables with the adjusters near the throttle grip. Then he pulls the carburetor off the intake manifold, and while holding it, unhooks the two cables, explaining as he does, "having slack in the cables makes this job much easier."

Now Ken removes the motor mount bracket and horn, then he takes out the spark plugs,

1. Exhaust comes off by removing the flange nuts first, then the nuts on the bracket (shown in upper photo).

2. Throttle cables come off more easily if you put some slack in the cables first.

3. After putting slack in the cables, Ken pops the carburetor out of the manifold and then unhooks the two carb cables.

4. Now the horn and upper motor mount are removed.

Note the MAP sensor is disconnected, and a special Allen wrench is being used to loosed the intake manifold bolts.

...followed by the rocker assemblies. Be sure the lifters are on the cam's base circle, which minimizes strain on the assembly during disassembly.

Ken takes the top of each rocker box off next...

With the rocker assemblies off, the lower rocker box is next. Ken warns, "don't lose the O-rings that go under the rocker assemblies."

...the breathers come off next...

Head bolts are loosened in a sequence, then the head and push rod tubes can be pulled off.

because, "with the plugs out it's easier to turn over the engine later in the process." The intake manifold is next. The map sensor is disconnected, then a special ball-end Allen wrench makes it easier to loosen the four Allen bolts.

ROCKER BOXES

As shown, Ken removes the top of the front cylinder box first, being careful to keep all the parts organized: with the front cylinder parts in one group and rear in another so they all go back together in the same group. It's time now to put a jack under the bike and turn the engine over until the intake closes. This leaves the front cylinder on the compression stroke and both lobes on the cam's base circle, which minimizes tension on the valve train during disassembly. Ken likes to put the eraser end of a pencil in the plug hole and roll the engine back and forth so he knows it's at TDC.

The breather covers come off now. Ken does the front cylinder first. The bolts for the lower rocker box are next. Ken rolls it over again so the rear cylinder has both cams on the base circle (compression or firing). The lower rocker box bolts for the rear cylinder come out now. Head bolts come out in a criss-cross sequence, as noted in the service manual, and then the heads are off. With the heads off the cylinders are next, followed by the lifter covers and the anti-rotation pins. "I always put the lifters on the bench in such a way that I can reinstall them the way they came out, not turned 180 degrees," explains Ken.

1. With the heads off Ken can lift off the cylinders as shown.

2. After removing the anti-rotation pins Ken pulls the lifters - which will be reinstalled in exactly the same position and orientation.

3. Be careful not to make a mess with the oil trapped behind the cover.

4. Here you see the tension unloader and retention pin described in the text.

With a socket wrench on the tool, Ken rotates the tensioner against spring tension and installs the pin. Removal of the primary chain and gears is next.

Before pressing the cams out of the support plate, Ken unloads the other tensioner and installs the second retention pin...

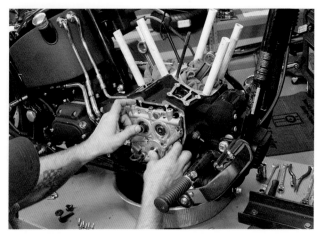

Once the primary cam chain and gears are out of the way, Ken removes the small machine bolts that hold the support plate and then the plate itself.

...and don't forget to remove the snap ring from the front camshaft.

Try to avoid having the oil pump come out with the cam support plate as it's removed.

Now the small retaining plate can be removed...

...and the cams can finally be pressed out of the support plate using the special tool shown here...

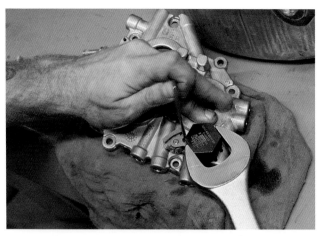

...now the retention pins can be removed.

At this point Ken pulls the cam cover and then uses a JIMS tool to crank back the tensioner and put the pin in place to hold it off. (Tool #1283-1 with 2 pins, note the nearby photos.) "Because I did the front first then the rear cylinder, and left rear at TDC, the timing marks are lined up, which is nice if a chain drive cam set up is going back in."

Once the retention pin is installed Ken can take off the primary drive chain and gears. Next he removes the six small machine screws positioned on the perimeter of the cam support plate. There are four more machines screws, the four that screw into the oil pump, that must be removed before the plate itself can be pulled out of the engine case.

"Try not to let the oil pump come out with the cam plate," warns Ken, "and try not to get oil on the clutch cable housing, it's fiber and will soak up the oil and drip on the ground later making it look like you've got an oil leak."

Before proceeding farther Ken installs the second retention pin, as shown on the facing page. Next he takes out the snap ring, then the retaining plate on the support plate's back side.

This is the bearing removal tool in place...

Press out Cams, Install New Bearings & Cams

Once the cams are pressed out (note the photos) it's time to pull the inner cam bearings, with JIMS tool #1279, "if this were getting a high lift cam I would pull the oil pump and clearance the case," adds Ken, "but these are just mild cams so we will just check the lobe-to-case clearance but should-

...and this is the tool and bearing after the bearing has been removed.

New bearings are installed with the tool shown here, be sure the writing is facing out, and put a little oil on the outside of the bearing.

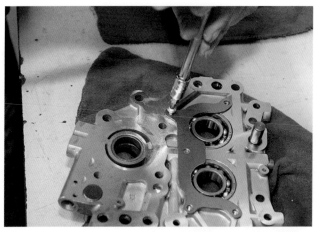

Small machine screws for the support plate are tightened to 20 to 30 in. lbs. It's a good idea to make sure later that the cam doesn't touch this plate.

Bearings are held in by a light interference fit - it's easy to tell when they're bottomed in the bore.

Lobe-to-case clearance should be checked between the cam and lifter bore, and the cam and case (behind the oil-pump).

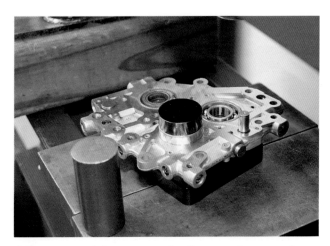

The press tool shown puts the force on the outer bearing race, and helps ensure the bearing goes in straight.

The gears must be installed on the new cams, be sure the keys are pressed ALL the way into the keyway first.

The cam gear needs to be carefully lined up before being pressed on or "the key will cut its own slot into the gear."

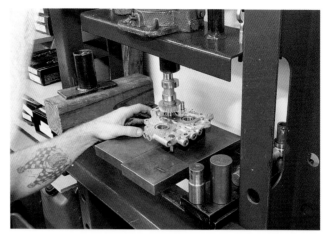

Ken pressed the new camshafts in individually...

n't have to do anything except clearance the outer cover (later). Now we drive in the new inner cam bearings with JIMS tool # 1278, as shown in the nearby photos.

Next the new cam bearings are pressed into the support plate with the installer tool as shown. Even though these are mild cams, Ken checks the clearance between the lobes and the case, and in this case there is plenty of clearance. Ken installs the retaining plate, applying a little blue Loctite to the small machine screws, each of which is tightened to 20 to 30 in. lbs.

The gears need to be installed on the camshafts, but first the keys must be installed in the cams as shown. The cams are not the same, the rear cam has a longer shaft because it connects to the outer gear.

With the gears on the cams, the cams themselves are pressed into the plate. This can be done two at a time, but Ken presses them in one at a time. It's important that they be timed correctly, as shown in the directions and the nearby photos. At this point we have a fully assembled cam support plate ready to be reinstalled into the engine case.

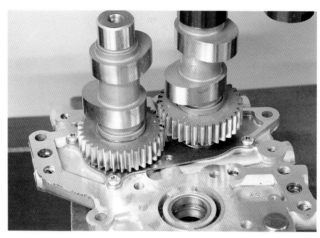

...when the second cam goes in you have to be sure the gears are aligned...

...as shown in this finished assembly. There are timing marks on the other side (the shaft side) as well.

It's easy to forget to install a new snap ring on the front camshaft.

This is the Evo lifter block alignment tool used to align the Twin Cam oil pump during assembly.

Here's the screen mentioned in the text, be sure it's clean and that a new O-ring is used.

The lower gear goes on first, pulled into place with a long bolt.

With the cams and components prelubed and new O-rings in place the cam support plate can be installed.

Then the correct bolt is installed with red Loctite and tightened to 25 ft. lbs.

There are three O-rings used between the cam plate and engine case, one for the oil pump and two for transfer ports between the case and the cam support plate. It's important to replace all the O-rings. Be sure to inspect the screen as shown on the facing page and clean as necessary. Only one camshaft, the front one, get's a snap ring to hold it in place.

Ken recommends cleaning the cam support plate bolts, and installing them with a little blue Loctite on the threads. He also puts prelube on cam lobes and some on the gears as well.

There are six outer screws that hold the cam support plate to the case, and four more that screw into the oil pump. Ken installs the outer fasteners first. "There's a tightening sequence for these bolts," explains Ken. "The factory lists the torque range as 90 to 120 in. lbs., but S&S recommends 95 in. lbs. because some of the holes, those with dowels, can be stripped at 120 in. lbs.

OIL PUMP ALIGNMENT

There is a specific alignment procedure for the four bolts in the center of the plate, the ones that screw into the oil pump. Though there's more than one way to do this, Ken uses a tapered tappet tool (used to align lifter blocks on Evos) in # 1 and #2 holes as shown, snugs them down, then snugs down the other two, then installs the other two machine screws, where the tapered pins were installed, and torques all four in the sequence shown in the service manual to 95 in. lbs.

PRIMARY CAM GEARS

To pull the lower gear onto the crankshaft, Ken uses a bolt and washer. Once the gear is in place, red Loctite is used on the correct bolt, which is tightened to 25 ft. lbs. By putting the bike in gear, and holding the rear brake, Ken is able to prevent the shaft from turning. What's left is to line up the timing marks and install the upper gear. Once again the gear is pulled onto the shaft. The bolt is the one supplied with the kit. When the real upper bolt is installed, it is first treated to red Loctite then tightened to 34 ft lbs.

The one place where there's nearly always a clearance problem when converting to gear-drive cams is the outer cover. As shown, the one rib needs to be ground away. The clearance can be double checked with a little clay and adjusted as necessary.

Like the cam gears, the primary gears must be timed at the time of installation.

Ken uses a Dremel tool to clearance the outer cam cover as shown.

Here you can see how clay can be used to check the clearance between the cover and the gear.

115

The lifters are reinstalled, followed by alignment pins. There are special tools available that hold the lifters in place so they don't have to be removed.

Once the rings are checked, and installed on the pistons, the pistons can be installed on the connecting rods.

The only way to be really sure there are no metal filings left in the cylinders is to wash them thoroughly with soap and hot water.

Ring compressors are available, but Ken chose to do this the old fashioned way.

Each of the two upper rings must be pushed straight down into the cylinder so the end gap can be checked with a feeler gauge.

We're moving now. After the cylinders are slipped down all the way, the head gaskets and heads are set in place.

The cover itself is installed with more of the small machine screws, tightened to 90 to 120 in. lbs.

INSTALL LIFTERS, PISTONS AND CYLINDERS

The lower case is fully assembled, it's time now to start on the cylinders and top end. Ken starts by installing the lifters and the anti-rotation pins, everything in exactly the same position as before.

Before installing any of the top-end parts, Ken washes the cylinders thoroughly with soapy water, then takes clean engine oil and a clean paper towel (no lint), and wipes and wipes them out until the towels come away clean. This leaves a light film of oil at the same time which is good because it will prevent flash rust if the cylinders are going to sit on the shelf for a little while before assembly.

Before installing the rings on the pistons we have to check ring end gap. The instructions that come with the kit list the minimum clearance as .003 inch per inch of cylinder diameter, or just under .012 inches for a 3.75 inch cylinder.

Ken warns that, "you have to be sure to follow the directions on installation of the rings as there is a top and bottom to the first and second ring. And the cutout on the top of the piston is bigger for the intake valve, so the pistons have to be oriented correctly. I always put assembly lube on the piston pins before I install them." Now the cylinders are installed down over the pistons and rings.

CYLINDERS

The front cylinder is set down first, then the rear, as shown nearby. Cylinder heads are next, followed by the pushrods tubes. Torque the head bolts, first to 120 - 144 in. lbs., then to 15 to 17 ft. lbs., following the sequence in the service manual. The final step is to turn each bolt an additional quarter turn. The lower rocker boxes are installed next, note the caption regarding the gasket position. The fasteners are tightened to 156 inch pounds. Be careful to put the longer bolts on the left side, and tighten per the sequence in the manual.

The pushrods are installed now, the longer ones are for the exhaust, (there are only 2 lengths), be sure to put pre-lube on the ends. There are three O-rings on the pushrod tubes, be sure to replace them. In the HD kits, the top is yellow, the middle is black, bottom is black too but "they are different enough that they're easily identifiable."

It's a good idea to put anti-seize on the threads of the head bolts, and a little oil under the head, in order to ensure accurate torque-wrench readings.

Be careful with these gaskets as there is definitely a right (shown) and a wrong way.

Because the heads are stock with stock springs, the lower rocker boxes can be installed without enlarging the spring pockets.

Once the heads and lower rocker boxes are in place, the pushrods can be installed.

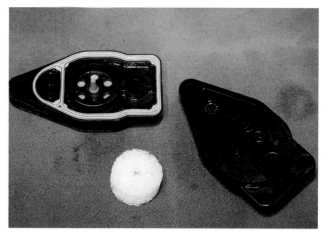

Breather assemblies get a new filter element.

Harley-Davidson makes shorter lower tubes, which is nice for adjustable pushrods as they slide up farther, making it easier to get at the adjuster.

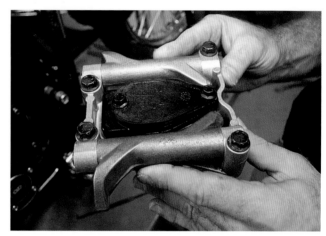

Now this rocker assembly is ready to install...

Don't forget the new O-ring under the rocker box assembly.

...as shown here.

The H-D tubes for adjustable push rods come with a shorter lower tube, which allows you to slide the tube up farther which provides more room to get at the adjusters. (H-D part #s: Lower Tube 17938-83. Upper chrome cover, 17634-9. Upper tube and the rest of the hardware stays the same. The complete kit is part # 17997-99A.)

Breather assemblies come in two styles, this is the one-piece design, which means the sponges (called a filter element) can be replaced, but not the rubber umbrella valves. With the new filter element in place the breathers can be dropped down onto rocker shaft assembly. Ken adds that "because these are adjustable pushrods, and they're collapsed all the way we aren't going to run the pistons up to TDC and get the cams on the base circle before tightening the bolts for the rocker shaft assemblies." The four bolts are tightened to 18 to 22 ft. lbs. in sequence and the breather bolts to 90 to 120 in. lbs.

REAR CYLINDER

Now it is necessary to run the first cylinder to be adjusted up onto the top of compression stroke (so the cams are on the base circle). The basic procedure is to adjust the pushrod to zero lash, then a certain number of turns after that. How many turns depends on the pitch of the threads, so each brand of pushrod is different. With the Crane adjustable push rods it's 2-1/2 turns after zero lash, which happens to be the same as H-D pushrods. Once Ken has one cylinder adjusted he lets those lifters bleed down (evidenced by the fact that you can rotate the pushrod with your fingers) before turning the engine over and going through the same procedure for the other cylinder.

CARBURETOR SET UP

To help the carburetor better meet the needs of the new hopped up engine, Ken gives it a quick tune up as follows:

Take off float bowl. Take out the slow-speed jet, Stock is 45 for all T-Cs. Start by going to a new slow jet, a number 48. Remove the cap for the idle mixture screw (ours was already removed). Ken starts with the screw 2-1/4 turns out from seated (stock is usually 1-1/2). The main jet is a 190, which Ken thinks is bigger than stock so he decides to leave it alone for now. Take off top cover and install a new needle. Be very careful that the

Ken uses an extension on the torque wrench to get at the plug-side push rod assembly bolts, "you don't have to compensate with the torque setting if the extension is 90 degrees to the axis of the wrench."

Adjustment is a matter of extending the pushrod until you obtain zero lash, then extending them a certain number of turns and tightening the jam nut.

Idle adjustment screw is at the top, slow jet lives at the bottom of the deep well, main jet is easily seen.

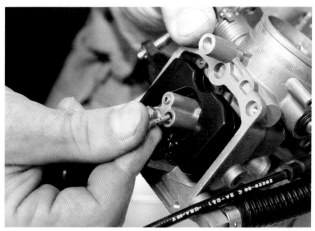

Here you can see the slow jet, located at the bottom of the cast tube as shown.

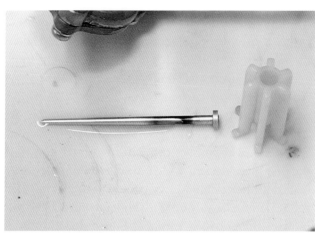

The needle, which is held in place by the plastic sleeve shown here, is changed as part of the carb upgrade.

The idle adjusting screw is inside this cast boss. Access is usually blocked by a brass plug.

Always use new O-rings on the intake manifold.

The tapered needle lives under the cover and under the plastic sleeve shown in the next photo.

This fixture is handy to keep the carb straight as the intake bolts are tightened. Once they're tight the carb will be popped out of the manifold one more time.

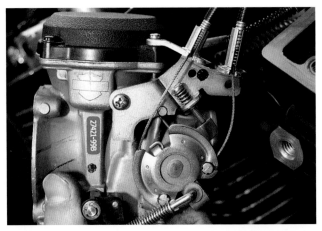

The return cable has a spring at the carburetor end, and goes in the inside position.

A hole-saw with a diameter just smaller than the weld is used...

diaphragm stays seated on the carb body, along the edge. The new needle is #27094 88, a 1200 Sporty needle.

Ken installs the intake manifold next, with the help of a fixture that will ensure the carburetor is sitting at the right angle before he does the final tightening of the intake manifold bolts. With the fixture in place the bolts are tightened almost all the way (they're still a little hard to get at). Then after the fixture is removed and the carburetor is popped out of the way, the bolts are double checked to be sure they are tight.

The throttle cables are installed now, with the cable adjusters still in the slack position (they are adjusted later). And then Ken can install the air cleaner, with some thread sealer on the breather bolts. The top motor mount is next, then the plug wires are connected to the new plugs.

To hang the exhaust, Ken gets the bracket on the studs first, then attaches the header flanges and tightens those, then tightens the nuts on the frame studs. Installing the exhaust is one of those things that needs to be done with a little finesse to make sure the parts are seated and positioned correctly. Our budget exhaust option is shown on the right, what might be called the high-tech hole-saw option.

What's left is to adjust the throttle cables, reinstall the tank, put in gas and oil and crank 'er up. To see just how much power our combination of parts actually makes, and ensure the carb is jetted correctly, we took the bike to the local dyno facility and that reports follows on the next page.

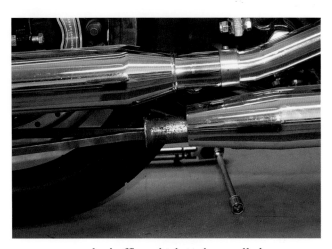

...to cut out the baffle, which is then pulled out as shown.

"I like to use the stock Harley clamps for the gas lines, they're a lot neater, and be sure to reinstall the vacuum line on the petcock, it's easy to forget."

A Dyno Day

At World Class Tuning, the dyno room is a former paint booth.

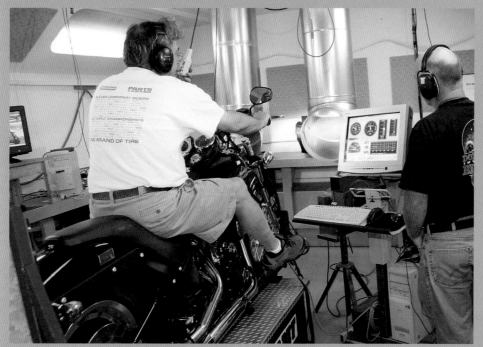

The first order of business is to get the bike well warmed up and just see how it runs.

To determine just how much horsepower and torque we obtained by installing the Kuryakyn 95 inch kit with their cams, and to ensure the air-fuel ratio and the timing are set at their optimum value, we took the Night Train to Doug Lofgren at World Class Tuning, in Watertown, Minnesota.

Doug starts out by positioning the bike on the dyno, attaching the dyno's computer to the bike's CPU with the data link, and attaching an inductive pickup on one plug wire. Next, it's a matter of running the bike through the gears repeatedly to get it thoroughly warmed up.

As Doug explains, "what's really important are the numbers. People get intimidated by the machinery and the computer, but it's the numbers that matter. What you need for good dyno work is consistency, repeatability. Once you get good consistent results then you can make changes based on small increments in power."

Dyno runs are done in 4th gear. Doug starts below 2000 rpm and rolls it open very quickly. The revs build fast and smooth all the way

A Dyno Day

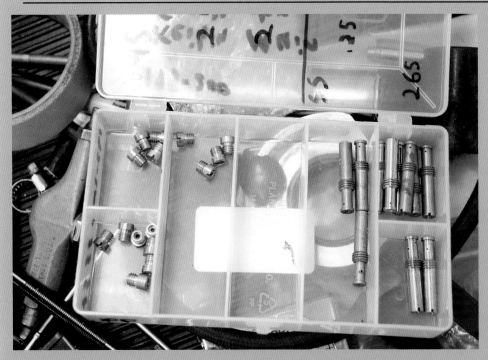

It takes a big box of jets, and some tiny drill bits, to properly tune a carbureted bike.

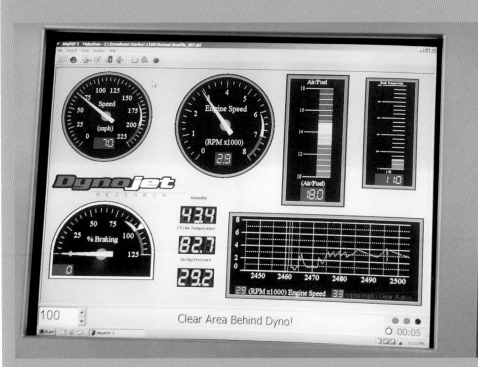

A huge variety of readouts can be chosen, this is the information Doug has available to him during the run.

to 5500, when the engine starts to break up. The numbers we get from the first few runs are 94 ft. lbs. of torque and nearly 86 horsepower. So even without any further tuning we're well up on a stock Twin Cam with about 65 horsepower.

At the bottom of the typical dyno chart is another graph, the air-fuel graph. An ideal air fuel ratio under full power is 13.1 to 1. In our case the numbers are more like 14.5 to 1, or way too lean. Doug decides to add a bigger main jet, "to richen the mixture all the way through the rpm range." To make a long story short, we go from a 190 to a 200, then start drilling the 200 until we're at a number 230 jet and have achieved a fairly flat, 13.1 to 1, fuel curve all the way to redline.

Speaking of redline, the reason the bike wouldn't run past 5500 is because the Twin Tech ignition module came with the rev limiter (and the ignition timing) set at a very conservative level. Near the end of the jetting sequence Doug begins to add timing as well.

A Dyno Day

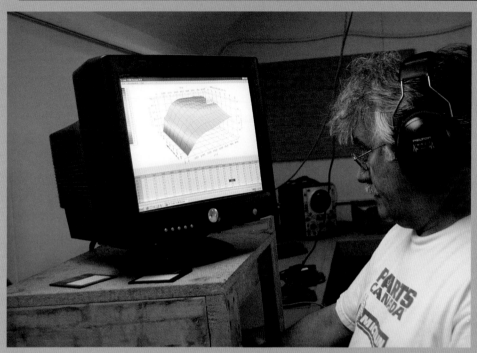

Here you can see one of the three-dimensional fuel maps from the Twin Tec Ignition. Individual points in the map can be changed, or the shape can be altered.

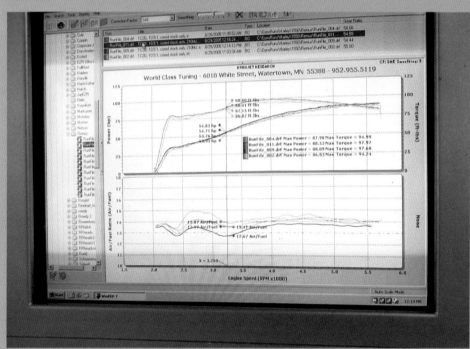

A screen shot of our initial dyno runs. Note the wavy air fuel line (at the bottom) especially between 2500 and 3500 rpm.

The first thing he did is set the rear cylinder to fire three degrees later than the front. The Twin Tech can be adjusted either by turning the small radial switches built into the unit, or by making much more sophisticated choices with the computer. Doug opts for option number two, which allows him to add or subtract timing, in very small increments, at any point in the rpm/speed/load map.

If you add too much timing the bike will ping or detonate, which can be heard even over the horrendous noise levels in the dyno room. But before reaching that level the additional timing will cause the power to drop off. As Doug explained near the end of our dyno run, "I gave it more timing throughout the rpm range and it didn't increase the max torque but the power came up a little. So I backed everything off two degrees and then added timing at the upper RPM range. The particular map we've loaded into this bike has the timing backed off at low rpm/low vacuum (high load) conditions so it won't ping when you roll it open on the street without

A Dyno Day

Before and after dyno charts. Basically we went from an untuned 86 and 94 horsepower and ft. lbs. of torque, to a finely tuned 89 and 98.

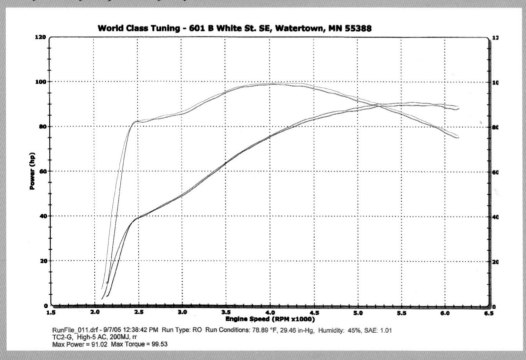

When we brought the bike back to try one of the new Kuryakyn air cleaners, we obtained another 2 horses - extra power doesn't come easy and there are no magic bullets.

downshifting."

All Doug's patient massaging of this particular V-twin nets us 98 ft. lbs. of torque and 89 horsepower. Again, not bad for what is essentially a budget hop up. As an aside, we came back another day and tried one of the new Kuryakyn Hi Five air cleaners which gave us an additional two horsepower for a total of 91. We should note that even the simple change from one high-flow air filter to another required re-jetting because, as Doug explained, "the air filter design affects how the air-flow travels over the vent for the float bowl, which in turn affects the float level." So, as always, nothing is simple and the best results go to those who pay attention along the way.

Chapter Nine

Softail Assembly

A Shadley Custom

The Heritage Softail has to be one of the best selling of all the Softail models sold by The Motor Company. In spite of the bike's classic good looks, sometimes a guy needs a little more - power, chrome and sex appeal. The sequence seen here involves the conversion of a 2002 Heritage from stock to modern mild custom. The work, performed at the Shadley Brothers shop in Whitman, Massachusetts, is designed to improve both the performance and looks without breaking the bank.

The owner of this Heritage wanted an upgrade not an overhaul. The project adds fresh paint, a cleaner look and more power without altering frame dimensions or diminishing the bike's strengths as a daily rider.

THE PLAN

The visual changes made to the Softail include some of what might be called "cleaning up the design," as well as more typical changes to the paint, headlight, taillight and blinkers. Though the stock sheet metal remains, the stock paint does not. Also included in the job are some chassis upgrades including a chrome swingarm, chrome brake calipers and lowering at both ends.

The clean up work, things like running the wires through the handle bars, is not included in the the photos. And because we have another start-to-finish engine sequence in this book, we've left off the conversion of this engine from 88 to 95 cubic inches. What we did include is everything else, from fork and chassis reassembly, to the flushing of the oil tank, to installation of the new clutch and throttle cables.

FRONT END ASSEMBLY

Our sequence starts with the reassembly of the fork. Mark Shadley believes that everything - from Chevy Trucks to Harley-Davidsons - looks better closer to the ground. To drop the front end Mark decided to use a Low Boy H-D lowering kit from White Bros. Installation of the kit, including new seals and a refill with fresh oil, is not covered, as we have another lowering sequence in Chapter Five.

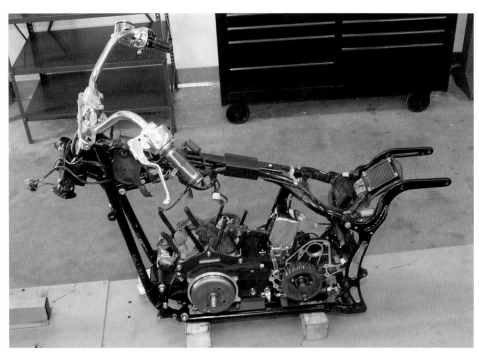

At Shadleys the bike was pulled down to an engine and frame. There's no point in going all the way to a bare frame if you don't have to.

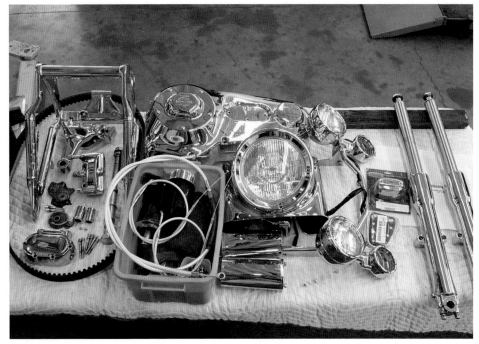

The parts going back on the bike are a combination of stock, stock with new chrome plate, and aftermarket. It's important to keep things organized so there's some chance you can find everything when it comes time for reassembly.

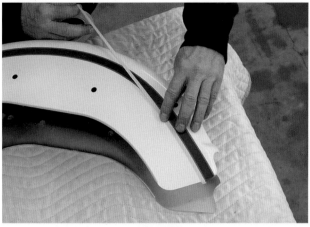

The base paint is a special white pearl mix from the Shadley paint department. John Hartnett is responsible for laying down the nice pinstripes.

John puts paint and thinner on a "palette." The idea is to get the paint to the right consistency and also work the paint up into all the bristles of the brush...

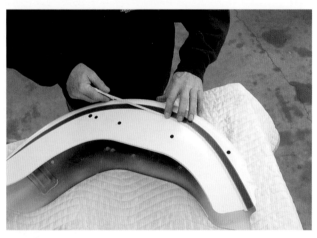

John runs a thin line of tape to establish the distance between the stripe and the pinstripe and to act as a guide for the pinstripe.

...so the brush holds enough paint to make a long continuous line without having to go back and pick up more paint.

The color is U15, lavender, urethane pinstripe paint from the House of Kolor thinned with the special striping reducer.

Note how John supports the paint brush with the outside fingers and his other hand.

Installation of the aftermarket early-style headlight nacelle is next. This straightforward operation is followed by another; installation of the light bar which is a Genuine Harley part, available in the accessory catalog.

CLUTCH CABLE AND RIGHT SIDE TRANSMISSION COVER

Before proceeding further, Mark and crew install the new braided clutch cable into the right side transmission cover, (check the photos, page 130). The ramp-and-ball arrangement converts the motion of the clutch lever into a compressing force that acts on the clutch assembly via the clutch release rod that runs from one side of the bike to the other. Once the right side transmission cover is in place it's time to route the clutch cable up to the bars and connect it to the lever itself. Final adjustment of the clutch cable won't happen until the clutch itself is fully installed.

PRIMARY ASSEMBLY

All Big Twin Harleys and aftermarket bikes connect the engine and separate transmission with a primary chain (or belt). Assembly of the primary drive and clutch starts with installation of the inner primary housing. If you're buying a new chrome inner primary, it's important to understand that some come preassembled with all the bushings and seals installed. Other aftermarket inner primaries come in a raw condition

Now that one side is finished, John can start on the other. After drying the pinstripe will be buried in multiple clearcoats. The H of K paint can be used with or without hardener. When the stripes are going to be clearcoated, most painters do not use the hardener as it isn't needed.

The other side of the frame, just before reassembly begins. This is also a good look at a Twin Cam frame, note the differences between this frame and the Evo frame on page 65.

The top nut and washer and dust shield will be needed as the fork tube assemblies are inserted in the triple trees.

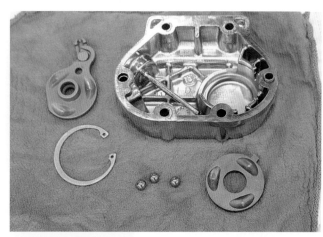

Before installing the new clutch release cover the release assembly and cable need to be installed.

Here Ed slips one of the tube assemblies in place. With this style of front end, be sure to attach the lower cans on the lower triple trees first.

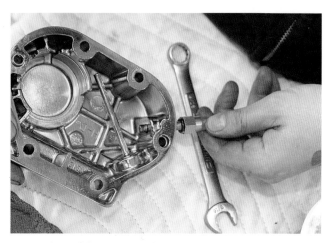

First the cable is screwed into place, Note the O-ring, some mechanics still put sealer on the cable housing threads, just in case.

The headlight nacelle is installed next.

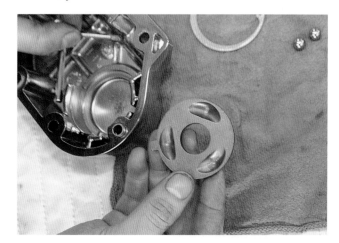

The outer ramp goes into the cover first.

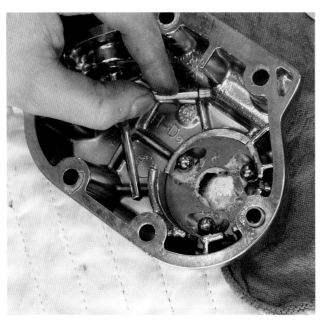

Next comes the three balls, all pre-lubed.

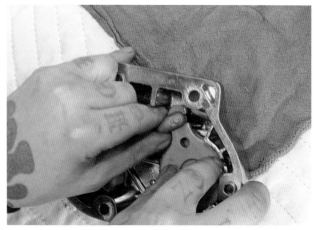

Now the inner ramp is connected to the cable, ...

...the inner ramp is held in place by the big snap ring...

... seen here again in the finished assembly.

requiring that you or the local shop, install the roller bearing and seal for the transmission shaft, and the bushing and seal for the starter.

Before installing the inner primary, Mark puts a little silicone on the back side where the bolts come through (see photos, next page), and on the lip where the inner meets the engine cases. Then the inner primary is installed and the bolts are snugged down. After allowing a little time for the silicone to set up, Mark pulls the bolts one at a time, puts red Loctite on the threads, and torques them down one at a time.

With the inner primary installed, Ed assembles the starter jackshaft assembly loosely and mounts it in the inner primary. Now the primary chain, compensator sprocket, and clutch assembly are pre-assembled and slipped up into place as an assembly. Once the primary drive is in place and both the compensator nut and clutch-hub-nut are snugged down, the drive assembly is checked for alignment. Even though the chain will tolerate a degree of mis-alignment, power is transmitted much more efficiently if the primary chain runs straight and true.

Mark turns the engine over a few revolutions by hand and then checks the alignment of the

Now the release cover can be installed with a new gasket. Next, Ed will route the cable to the control. It's a good idea to lube the cables before installation.

Here you can see silicone being placed on the back side of inner primary where the bolts come through. Be sure to put lube on the bearing and seal as well.

The cable is connected to the control, then the lever is slipped up into place. The boys in the shop all agree, "always pre-lube cables and pivots."

The primary bolts are torqued to 17 to 21 ft lbs. Be sure to put the drive belt on before inner primary (don't laugh). After the inner primary bolts are fully torqued, the lock tabs are bent over bolt heads.

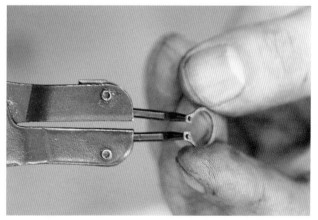

The pivot pin is held in place with the small snap ring shown here.

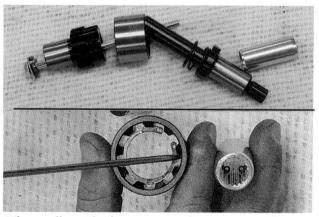

The small coupler has a counter bore on one end, which should face the jackshaft, not the starter. The bigger coupler has a shallow and deep side, shallow side should intersect with the teeth on the jackshaft.

chain. With a straight edge across the chain (as shown), first just behind the compensator sprocket, and then in front of the clutch hub, Mark checks the clearance between the inside of the straight edge and the gasket surface of the inner primary. The service manual states the allowable difference between the two readings to be .030 inches, but Mark likes to see the alignment off no more than .015 inches.

In this case Mark replaces the .130 inch shim located behind the compensator sprocket with a .120 inch shim, reassembles the whole thing and checks it again. The difference the second time is .005 inches, which is close to ideal.

The final assembly includes torquing the compensator nut and clutch-hub nut. The specification for the compensator is 150-165 ft., lbs. but most mechanics would replace the numbers with the words, "very tight." The factory makes a holding fixture so the engine won't turn over as you torque the nut, but in the real world most bike builders use their best impact wrench and red Loctite. In the case of the clutch-hub nut however the specification is 50 ft. lbs. and mechanics warn that the nut (a left-hand thread) should not be over-tightened.

With the primary assembly in place the chain is adjusted to 5/8-7/8 inch of play with a cold engine. The plastic shoe is adjusted up or down to adjust the play. Note the photos, there is a right and wrong way to install the shoe. Note number two, chain adjustment is one of those things that should be inspected during the 1000 mile check.

Before the assembly of the bike gets too far along, Ed and Jason line up the swingarm (newly chrome plated) and install it in the frame.

The clutch release rod slips inside the mainshaft next, with a little lube on both ends, followed by the adjuster assembly. The release plate is held in place with a snap ring, and once in place the screw can be turned in until it just touches the release rod (zero play) and then backed off one-half turn. This is the initial clutch adjustment, the final adjustment will be done with the cable as shown in the nearby photos.

The starter drive assembly goes in from the outside....

...then the primary drive assembly can be slipped up into place.

The chain alignment needs to be checked at both the front and the back by inserting a feeler gauge between the straight edge and the edge of the inner primary.

In this case the chain is farther out at the front than the rear.

Ed installs the chrome plated swingarm at this point. The pivot bolts should be tightened to 90 ft. lbs.(be sure to use red Loctite).

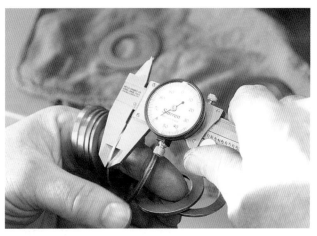

The washer that goes between the compensator sprocket assembly and the rotor is available in different thicknesses.

A little lube is placed on the adjusting screw, where it goes up against the clutch push rod. This stops the rod from galling.

The plastic shoe is moved up or down until the cold primary chain has 5/8 to 7/8 inches of up and down play.

The release plate, complete with adjusting screw and lock nut, is held in place with a large snap ring.

2). Final clutch adjustment is done with the cable adjuster. Cable is adjusted to achieve the right amount of free play between clutch lever and clutch perch.

INSTALL STARTER MOTOR

The starter motor is brought in from the right side, at this point the pinion assembly is already hanging from the inner primary on the other side. Be sure the jack shaft components are assembled correctly, (note detail photo on a preceding page) and that the small coupler is in place on the end of the starter before you slide it into place. The jackshaft bolt is final-tightened to 84 to 108 in. lbs. after the starter is final-tightened.

INSTALL THE FRONT WHEEL

Installation of the front wheel is pretty simple, and made even easier if the bike can be jacked up so the wheel can simply be rolled into place, then the axle, with the proper spacers, can be slipped into place and tightened per the nearby photos. An extra set of hands is helpful to hold spacers while the axle is slipped through the lower leg and hub. Owners of older Softails, with non-sealed bearings, will have the additional task of checking and adjusting the wheel bearing end play. Before finishing up the front end, Ed installs the chrome plated factory caliper with new crush (sealing) washers. Some builders like the washers ringed by neoprene as they seal more easily (not shown). Whatever you use, don't re-use the old washers and be sure to check for leaks after bleeding.

1). The adjusting screw is turned in until it lightly touches the push rod, then backed out one half to one turn and locked down with the lock nut as shown. This is the initial clutch adjustment.

3). You need 1/16 to 1/8 inch of free play between the housing and the lever. Without some free play the force of the pressure plate is not fully applied to the clutch plates.

4). Now the starter is slipped into place, engaged with the drive assembly (already installed) and left hanging loose to make oil tank installation easier.

Coated with anti-seize the axle is slipped into place. Because this is the stock wheel/fork the spacers are the same ones Ed and Jason took out on disassembly.

Most aftermarket braided hoses are designed to accept a wide variety of ends to fit nearly any situation. Be sure to check for leaks later.

The slider nuts (left) are snugged down enough so the axle won't turn, then the axle nut is fully tightened (red Loctite), and the slider nuts are loosened and re-tightened to the final toque spec.

Bleeding is done with a Phoenix injector pump that pushes fluid in at the bleeder until the reservoir is filled. A little hand bleeding may still be needed.

More red Loctite. When stock caliper bolts are replaced be sure the new bolts are Grade 8, and that they aren't so long they can hit the rotor.

The two cables are not the same, and install as shown. The housings are replaced at the same time.

BLEED BRAKE, FRONT

Bleeding is done with a system that pushes fluid through from the bleeder. "This doesn't solve all your problems," adds Jason, "but it eliminates some of them. You still might have to get it down off the hoist and lean the bike over to get rid of all the air bubbles. I hold the fitting onto the bleeder, and pump real slow, because it's a new line and empty master, it will take a while, there's a lot of air in there."

THROTTLE CABLES

Ed and Jason decide to finish up the installation of the throttle cables at this time. Jason points out two notable details, "The cable with a spring on the 'carburetor' end is idle cable, and be careful that you don't lose the little brass cable ends." It's a good idea to lube them first. Idle cable goes on the outside, note photos. "Set the throttle cable first," explains Jason, "to get a fully open throttle. Then use the adjustment on the idle cable to take almost all the slack out of the grip. Be careful to check the cables when the bike is off the hoist, turn the bars both ways and make sure there's still slack at idle, you don't want to all of a sudden open the throttle when you go into a curve."

SHEET METAL, LIGHTS AND WIRING
Oil Tank Install

Installation of the oil tank is like everything else about a custom bike, more work than you think it ought to be. The process starts as Jason runs a tap into all the holes. Next the paint is scraped off the mounting surfaces so the paint doesn't "squeeze out" after the bike is assembled. To clean the crud out of the tank the boys first blow it out with compressed air, then put it in parts cleaner for hours, followed by a multi-step rinse with hot water, another blow-job and another rinse with a bit of denatured alcohol to absorb any lingering water.

The actual mounting of the tank starts with a towel placed over the starter to avoid scratches. Before sliding the tank into place the coil and coil center post are taken out of the way. The back bolts are installed first, followed by the upper L bracket and bolts (the oil drain line was put on earlier). Jason tightens all the brackets gradually,

The small brass ferrules need to be attached to the ends of the cables...

...before the cables are attached to the grip as shown.

Here you see the correct routing of the cables at the throttle body.

The gizmo shown mounted to the cable is designed to funnel oil from a can of WD-40, or similar lube, to the inner cable.

Once cleaned and flushed the oil tank can be installed into the frame – and the starter bolts fully tightened.

Most mechanics start off with the adjusters (shown) set to provide plenty of slack in the cables, which is eliminated once the cables are installed.

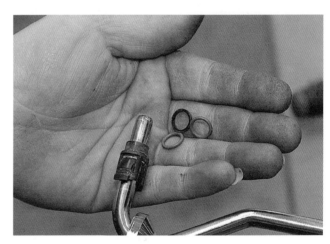

Oil lines snap into the tank, new O-rings are a good idea here.

Preparing the oil tank for installation means sanding off excess paint and running a tap into threaded female fittings.

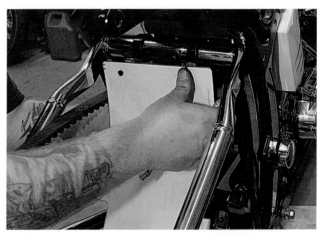

The new splash shield was passed through a set of rollers at a sheet metal shop to provide a nice even radius before being installed.

making sure as he does that everything fits together nicely.

The starter bolts were left loose so the starter would hang down just a little, those two fasteners are tightened up now before the oil lines are installed. The newer oil lines seal with O-rings, those on the engine are re-used (they're usually not much of a problem). Some of the lines aren't installed until later in the project.

Rear splash shield and Fender

Before the newly shaped splash shield is installed, the small aftermarket horn is hidden on the front side. When it comes to wiring the light, Mark explains that, "You can either try to decipher the color codes from the factory manual, or you can just plug the harness into the plug near the battery, and then use a test light to figure out which wire is which." The rear fender was modified for the tombstone light, blinkers are a Harley-Davidson part and bolt right on.

REAR WHEEL

Once the fender is in place the rear wheel is rolled into place (with the bike jacked up), then the bike is lowered and the caliper is slipped into place.

Jason slides the axle in from the left, explaining, "that way you can change a tire without having to pull off the exhaust." This particular model uses two rear wheel spacers. "The bigger one is always on the left," explains Jason, "the small one goes in on the right between caliper and the hub. For alignment, I get it close by eye, and then I use a tape measure to make sure the axle is in the same position from one side to the other with the belt at the right tension."

The front fender is a pretty simple piece to install, with chrome Allens, a washer and Nylock nuts.

THE FLUSH JOB

After being flushed in a manner similar to that used for the oil tank, the external fuel fitting is installed into the bottom of the gas tank. The hose from this fitting attaches to the output fitting on the electronic fuel pump assembly that resides inside the tank. The assembly is hinged to make reinstallation easier. If in doubt, be sure to use a

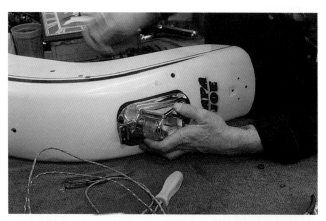

Installing the tombstone taillight meant bolting it on, marking the gasket, pulling it apart, trimming the gasket and then re-installing the light. Wiring is done with butt connectors because ...

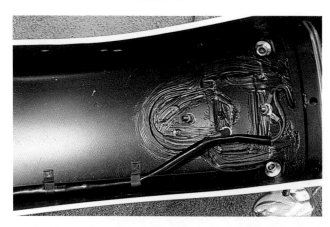

... "solder makes the wire brittle and it can break." Shrink wrap is used along with factory sheathing to make a clean, neat harness, When fenders, seats or lights are bolted on be sure the studs and wiring...

...can't get anywhere near the tire. Factory harness colors are: Blue, power to the taillight. Orange w-white, running light. Red w-yellow, brake. Black, ground. Brown, right turn. Purple, left turn.

Install the axle from the left side, "so you can take the wheel off without taking off the muffler." Inset shows small spacer between wheel and caliper carrier.

The outlet fitting and hose are screwed into the bottom of the tank. The hose from the outlet fitting attaches to fuel pump assembly...

Adjusters shown here are used to adjust wheel so it's straight in the frame and belt tension is correct. The axle nut is tightened to 60 to 65 ft. lbs.

... then the assembly is slipped back into the tank. The gasket should be new, and seal against bare steel.

Front fender is installed using chrome Allen bolts (shown) and Nylock nuts so the bolts can't come loose. Bolt-to-tire clearance should be checked.

Mark does a light dyno run to ensure the engine runs OK and that the fuel mixture is close. Then some break-in miles and the final dyno runs.

new gasket between the tank and fuel pump assembly and be sure the gasket itself sits on bare metal, not paint.

The tank itself is held in place with one through bolt at the front, and one bolt at the rear. The three wires that emerge from the bottom of the tank go to the plug under the tank, for the fuel gauge. The wires have to be slipped back into the plug, then the two plugs can be mated. The dash and ignition switch are a plug and play deal, the dash is held in place with a single fastener.

For exhaust Mark chose V&H pipes, and everything fits good. In order to ensure the exhaust is installed correctly without a lot of tension on the brackets or pipes, Jason and Ed follow a set sequence.

1. With a helper, get the exhaust hanging loose on the bike. 2. Get the flanges set over the studs. 3. Start nuts on all four studs, snug each nut down gently. 4. Put bolts in the rear bracket, but do not tighten. 5. Tighten up the flange nuts gradually. 6. Tighten up the bracket bolts. 7. The outside chrome covers go on last. Jason uses the smaller header gaskets (not shown) for better performance.

There are early and late model Softail seats, the Twin Cam models use the later seat. At this point the bike is nearly finished. The boys add oil and primary fluid, cycle the fuel pump a few times by turning the ignition on and off, and finally hit the starter button. The bike fires right away. Mark lets it run for two minutes before shutting it off. After cooling he lets it run for five minutes the next time. Once he's cycled the bike through a few run and cool cycles, Mark does a short dyno run under only partial power, to ensure the bike runs good and isn't lean.

Mark likes to get at least 500 miles on the bike before doing the final dyno runs. Those final runs on the Shadley Brothers dyno are done later with a Power Commander to remap the factory fuel injection. The best run nets them 104 ft. lbs. and 94 horsepower.

The 95 inch engine uses Jerry Branch heads, Andrews 37B chain-drive cams, flat-top pistons and the V&H pipes.

The exhaust pipes are from V&H, the air cleaner from Arlen Ness. The finished machine looks far different from stock, while still retaining the basic good looks and nice lines that a Heritage Softail is known for.

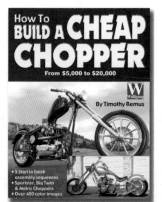

HOW TO BUILD A CHEAP CHOPPER

Choppers don't have to cost $30,000.00. In fact, a chopper built at home can be had for as little as $5,000.00. Watch the construction of 4 inexpensive choppers with complete start-to-finish photo sequences. Least expensive are metric choppers, based on a 1970s vintage Japanese four-cylinder drivetrain installed in an hardtail frame. Next up are three bikes built using Buell/Sportster drivetrains. The fact is, a complete used Buell or Sportster is an inexpensive motorcycle -- and comes with wheels and tires, transmission, brakes and all the rest. Just add a hardtail frame and accessories to suit. Most expensive is bike number 4. This big-twin chopper uses a RevTech drivetrain set in a Rolling Thunder frame. Written by Tim Remus. Shot in the shops of Brian Klock, Motorcycle Works, Redneck Engineering and Dave Perewitz this book uses numerous photos to Illustrate the construction of these 4 bikes.

Eleven Chapters   144 Pages $24.95   Over 400 photos-100% color

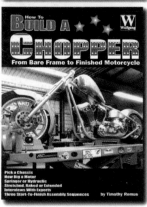

HOW TO BUILD A CHOPPER

Designed to help you build your own chopper, this book covers History, Frames, Chassis Components, Wheels and Tires, Engine Options, Drivetrains, Wiring, Sheet Metal and Hardware. Included are assembly sequences from the Arlen Ness, Donnie Smith and American Thunder shops. Your best first step! Order today.

Choppers are back! Learn from the best how to build yours.
12 chapters cover:
• Use of Evo, TC, Shovel, Pan or Knucklehead engines
• Frame and running gear choices
• Design decisions - short and stubby or long and radical?
• Four, five or six-speed trannies

Twelve Chapters   144 Pages $24.95   Over 300 photos-over 50% color

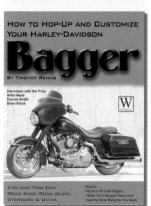

HOP-UP & CUSTOMIZE YOUR H-D BAGGER

Baggers don't have to be slow, and they don't have to look like every other Dresser in the parking lot. Take your Bagger from slow to show with a few more cubic inches, a little paint and some well placed accessories. Whether you're looking for additional power or more visual pizazz, the answers and ideas you need are contained in this new book from Tim Remus.

Follow the project bike from start to finish, including a complete dyno test and remapping of the fuel injections. Includes two 95 inch engine make overs.
How to:
• Pick the best accessories for the best value
• Install a lowering kit
• Do custom paint on a budget
• Create a unique design for your bike

Eight Chapters   144 Pages $24.95   Over 400 full-color photos

ADVANCED AIRBRUSH ART

Like a video done with still photography, this new book is made up entirely of photo sequences that illustrate each small step in the creation of an airbrushed masterpiece. Watch as well-known masters like Vince Goodeve, Chris Cruz, Steve Wizard and Nick Pastura start with a sketch and end with a NASCAR helmet or motorcycle tank covered with graphics, murals, pinups or all of the above.

Interviews explain each artist's preference for paint and equipment, and secrets learned over decades of painting. Projects include a chrome eagle surrounded by reality flames, a series of murals, and a variety of graphic designs.
This is a great book for anyone who takes their airbrushing seriously and wants to learn more.

Ten Chapters   144 Pages $24.95   Over 400 photos, 100% color